7 October 2001 – 30 August 2021:
AFGHANISTAN

7 October 2001 – 30 August 2021:
AFGHANISTAN

Michael Kerrigan

amber
BOOKS

Published by Amber Books Ltd
United House
London N7 9DP
United Kingdom
www.amberbooks.co.uk
Facebook: amberbooks
Instagram: amberbooksltd
Twitter: @amberbooks
Pinterest: amberbooksltd

ISBN: 978-1-83886-317-3

Editor: Michael Spilling
Designer: Mark Batley
Picture research: Adam Gnych

Printed in Malaysia

Contents

Introduction

Afghanistan is ravishingly beautiful, with breathtaking vistas over mountain heights and plunging valleys; open hillsides cut by tumbling streams; and empty plains punctuated by little villages and compounds. However, its beauty is austere and its scenery spare, with much of its appeal lying in the romance of the wild. Its people are, by common consent, as unyielding as their homeland.

The country has frequently been characterized as 'unconquerable'. This would have been news not only to Macedonia's Alexander the Great, who occupied Afghanistan in the 4th century BCE, but also to the Indian Mauryan Empire, which took the territory from his successors, and to the Sassanians who seized it a few generations later. So it continued, the country falling under the imperial control of (among others) the Huns in the 6th century CE; the Arabs (bringing Islam with them)

in the 7th century; the Mongols in the 13th century and the Turkoman Afsharids in the 18th century.

There is a degree of justification for the claim. None of these powers found the conquest of Afghanistan easy and all came badly unstuck there at one time or another. It's also only fair to stress that these conquerors generally didn't put down much of a 'footprint' there in terms of physical – or even institutional – infrastructure. They took the country without ever really taking full possession.

EASY-GOING EMPIRES

Yet this reflected the realities of life in much of Central and Western Asia throughout these periods. Most of the conquerors listed here were nomads. They didn't expect to establish anything more than the loosest of hegemonies over the lands they conquered. If they had the allegiance of local warlords, they were content.

This would not be good enough for the Western powers of more modern times. The colonial project only made sense if a high degree of imperial control could be established. For sustained development to take place, political stability had to be established from top to bottom of society. Having a few warlords onside simply would not suffice. Then there was the issue of the country's 'landlocked' status. The steady stream of conquerors that passed through in earlier periods had reflected Afghanistan's location at the centre of the Silk Road, which for centuries carried trade between China, Central Asia and the West. Only after the European states had started 'opening up' the world with ocean-going trade would the country's lack of a coastline come to be seen as a problem.

This, then, was the context in which Afghanistan became the 'graveyard of empires'. It wasn't readily reachable – either physically or

ABOVE:
BATTLE OF ALI MASJID
A group of British officers in 1878 prior to the Battle of Ali Masjid; three Afghans sit at the back. The opening encounter of the Second Anglo-Afghan War (1878–80) set the tone for the whole conflict. Britain won the battle, as they would the war. Defeating the uncooperative Emir Ayub Khan, they installed their puppet Abdur Rahman Khan, to usher in two decades of stability and peace – from the British point of view, that is. The emir brought his Afghan subjects a reign of tyranny, with 100,000 judicial executions and countless further deaths from famine and disease.

OPPOSITE:
'REMNANTS OF AN ARMY'
Assistant Surgeon William Brydon – reportedly the sole survivor of the Kabul garrison forced to a humiliating retreat in January 1842 – makes it to the safety of Jalalabad in a painting by Elizabeth Thompson. While this famous painting fostered sympathy for the idea of the 'white man's burden', it also helped cement the reputation of Afghanistan as the 'graveyard of empires'. As previous occupiers had learned, it was one thing to take the country; another to control it effectively. Earlier conquerors, however, had been content to keep it on a looser rein. Nomadic fighters themselves, they'd offered a less obvious target for resistance than modern occupiers, whose superior 'strength' often proved a liability.

mentally – to the modern European colonial powers. A mystique arose around this, although the reality was simple: Western governments never really found a focus for the country.

On the one hand, there was little reason to as the territory was worth little in itself. On the other hand, it was strategically vital. As Britain and Russia (and, more peripherally, France and the Ottoman Empire) came into competition over richer lands such as India and Persia, they tussled tactically in what became known as the 'Great Game'. A succession of diplomatic initiatives and (largely) small-scale military struggles with local proxies were interspersed with occasional bouts of cooperation. While the chessboard stretched from the Iranian marshes to the mountains of Tibet, Afghanistan was very much its centre.

The 'game' was already well under way when, in 1839, local ruler Dost Muhammad responded to British bullying by striking a new alliance with Russia. Britain sent 20,000 troops over the mountains to Kabul. Having

taken the city with ease, they left it garrisoned with 8000 troops. This was where the 'graveyard of empires' myth – that wasn't quite a myth – began. Over the ensuing months, diehard Dost Muhammad supporters started fighting back; with them fought a fair few opportunists. Traditionally, Afghans' loyalties had been to their warlords, whose own allegiances were ever-shifting.

Although much the stronger force, the British weren't equipped for a guerrilla war. In the absence of relief, they were forced to retreat – a hellish journey at the mercy of winter weather and persistent rebel attacks. Of the 16,000 (4500 soldiers; 11,500 servants) who had left Kabul, only one European and a handful of Indian soldiers made it back to Jalalabad, in eastern Afghanistan, still then securely held by British forces.

Two world wars and a Russian Revolution later, Afghanistan had remained the same in some respects. Not least in its significance strategically, but also in its waywardness, as

Russia's Soviet rulers were to discover in 1978, when local mujahideen guerrillas – fired by a volatile mix of patriotic and Islamic religious fervour – rose up against the client regime the USSR had established there.

SOVIET INVASION

At the end of 1979, the USSR invaded Afghanistan. Yet Soviet forces found themselves facing the same challenge the British had a century before. Despite their overwhelming military strength, they struggled to prevail.

Humbled itself a few years earlier in similar circumstances in Vietnam, the United States could hardly credit its good fortune. The schadenfreude was satisfying in itself, but the sight of its enemy in so much difficulty held out the more serious prospect of an end to three decades-plus of Cold War. The USA accordingly plied the mujahideen with weaponry, equipment and money, an immeasurable boon to the Afghan rebel cause.

ABOVE:
WHITE HOUSE APPROVAL
Mujahideen leaders enjoy the hospitality of US President Ronald Reagan in the White House. They were feted by Western leaders who felt that their Soviet enemy's enemy must be their friend. The assumption would prove time-limited. Culturally, religiously and in their formative experience of a life of fighting, these men could never really be the Western allies that they seemed.

OPPOSITE:
THIRD ANGLO-AFGHAN WAR
Afghans shoot from the Khyber Pass during the Third Anglo-Afghan War. In 1919, having taken power as Emir of Afghanistan, Amanullah Khan sought to shore up his power by mounting an invasion of British India. It wasn't so self-evidently foolhardy a venture as it might sound. British forces had been depleted by the demands of World War I, while there was serious discontent among those that remained. The invasion was repulsed, but Amanullah Khan's position was still strengthened.

More ominously for the longer term, they facilitated the development of a radical Islamist ideology and the structures of an international underground that were going to come back to haunt them in a few years' time.

A STING IN THE TAIL
A mujahideen fighter hefts an FIM-92 Stinger launcher on his shoulder during the Battle for Jalalabad in 1989. The US-made, portable, surface-to-air missile became the signature weapon of the Afghan resistance in the late 1980s. Soviet air power had up until 1985 given the invaders an inestimable advantage, but the arrival of the Stinger changed everything.

In hindsight, we can recognize a sort of shadow conflict gradually unfolding within the violent back and forth of the Afghan–Soviet War. And a complex one at that: America was by no means the only international player with an interest in stoking the conflict. Pakistan and Iran both supported the mujahideen not only because they wanted to see their neighbour-nation Afghanistan weakened, but because a compromised Soviet Union suited them in some ways too.

As it did China which, despite its Communist allegiances, felt dominated by the Soviets and was happy to do its bit for their discomfiture. For China also, this support was going to bring unwelcome blowback when the Islamic separatist movement took hold in the Xianjiang Uygur Autonomous Region a few years later.

SHADOW CONFLICT

However, the intervention of 'state actors' wasn't to be the most troubling feature of this shadow conflict – even if, again, this would only become evident in hindsight. Governments have to at least go through the motions of showing themselves accountable. Private individuals can act as they please,

OPPOSITE:
OSAMA BIN LADEN
The face that launched a thousand missiles. Eventually, Osama bin Laden would be among the world's most recognizable men. For now he was working incognito in Afghanistan. Despite his notoriety – and undoubted ruthlessness – his great skills were as a financier, raising and moving money for the mujahideen.

BELOW:
'THE LION OF PANJSHIR'
Commander Ahmad Shah Massoud gives orders to his officers in his headquarters in Charikar during peace negotiations with the communist government, after the departure of Soviet soldiers.

ABOVE:
SOVIET WITHDRAWAL
A convoy of Soviet armoured personnel carriers makes its way across a bridge at Termez on 21 May 1988, marking the start of a phased withdrawal that would take almost a year. The soldiers don't appear downcast in defeat – for them the war was over. For the beleaguered Afghans, the conflict would go on and on.

without fear of question – especially when backed by all but limitless private funds.

As the 1980s wore on, 'Afghan Arabs' arrived in their thousands. They came from every corner of the Arab world to defend Islam. Like those Western leftists of the 1930s who had flocked to fight for the Republic during the Spanish Civil War, they were driven by idealism – and, of course, a yearning for adventure. Mostly they came in the second half of the decade, by which time it had become obvious that the Soviets were going to have to leave.

Increasingly, however, it was clear that Islamism itself had become the cause and the Afghan War only the furnace in which it would be forged. The Soviet Union didn't

simply abandon its client: it continued to support the Republic of Afghanistan with arms, advice and copious economic aid. Under the leadership of Muhammad Najibullah, this socialist state struggled gamely on against the advancing mujahideen in what had now become an Afghan Civil War.

However, the USSR had been struggling too: its economy in ruins; its government in disarray; its Iron Curtain 'allies' in revolt. On 26 December 1991, the Soviet Union was formally dissolved. The Afghan government's only ally – sole underwriter of its abject economy – had literally ceased to exist. Running on empty, the Republic of Afghanistan staggered on for a few weeks longer, but on 15 February Najibullah agreed to stand down. Talks were held among the victorious mujahideen, and on 24 April a group of leaders signed the Peshawar Accord. The Islamic State of Afghanistan was proclaimed and an interim government installed.

One civil war segued straight into another when the Hezb-e Islami Gulbuddin group refused to recognize the new state. Armed by the Inter-Services Intelligence (ISI) agency of Pakistan – always eager to sow dissension among its neighbours – it mounted a major offensive against Kabul.

By June 1992, its fighters were dug in around the Afghan capital, which they subjected to a fierce artillery bombardment over many weeks. Much of the city was levelled and up to 50,000 people killed – mostly civilians. Afghanistan's sufferings, it seemed, were far from over.

STUDENT RADICALS

In fact, they were about to get a good deal worse. By 1994, a new threat was emerging among the Pashtun tribes of eastern and southeastern Afghanistan. Fundamentalist in their reading of Islam and puritanical in their moral attitudes, this group was calling for a wholesale transformation of Afghan society. The name they gave themselves – the 'Taliban' – translates literally as 'students'. They regarded themselves as scholars of the Quran after their training in special madrasas – traditional Islamic schools – across the border in western Pakistan.

The Taliban received more secular support from Pakistan as well, supplanting the Hezb-e Islami Gulbuddin as the ISI's chosen instrument for mischief-making. By 1996, with some three-quarters of the country under their control, the Taliban were in a position to establish what they called the First Islamic Emirate of Afghanistan.

Its people were condemned to rule by religious fanaticism. The Taliban prohibited music and the arts, most social activities and sport. Girls and women were harshly oppressed, barred from the worlds of work and education and forced to wear burkhas in public. Adultery was punishable by public flogging – and extremely broadly defined it included women simply being seen out in public with unrelated males.

BELOW:
TALIBAN TERRITORY
History was to repeat itself in Afghanistan between 2013 and 2021, although the Taliban's second tenure would prove as tragic as the first. Just as they had in the 1990s, they expanded out of isolated pockets in the Pashtun areas of the south and east, gradually extending their ascendancy over the country as a whole. For most of this time, the Taliban leadership directed operations from Pakistan. (They had a headquarters in the city of Quetta, near the Afghan border.) In the areas they controlled, they reintroduced their own rigorous brand of sharia law.

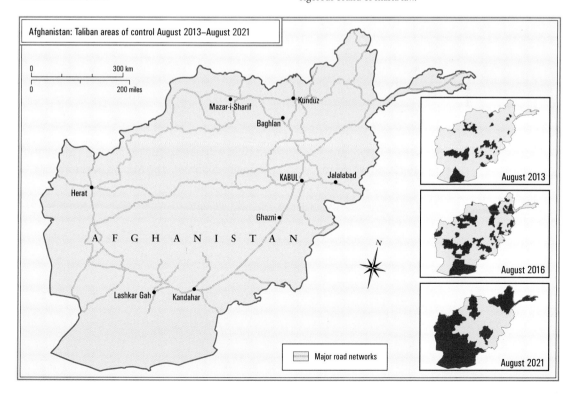

TERROR ATTACK

'Out of a clear blue sky,' they said and it soon became the defining cliché of '9/11'. The shock, however, was deepened by it all unfolding in slow motion. For a full 17 minutes after American Airlines Flight 11 hit the North Tower of the World Trade Center, at 8.46 a.m. Eastern time on 11 September 2001, it was assumed to have been a fearful but freakish accident.

This being Manhattan in the 21st century, there had been television crews in close proximity. Within two minutes, news footage was being broadcast live. Therefore the world was watching when, at 9.03, the impact of a second plane into the South Tower threw that of the first into a new perspective, transforming a disaster into an outrage. Like the first plane, United Airlines Flight 175 was a Boeing 767 out of Boston, bound for Los Angeles.

By 9.37, after American Airlines Flight 77, newly departed from Dulles Airport for Los Angeles, had hit the Pentagon, headquarters of the US defence establishment, it was clear that the country was under concerted attack. US airspace was shut down at 9.45 a.m. and all aircraft currently in flight were ordered to land.

OPPOSITE:
WORLD WARNING
The sight of the Twin Towers up in flames sent out the message that the reach of terror extended everywhere – even to the very heart of the global financial system.

LEFT:

HORROR STRUCK

Bystanders in the streets below could only look up in horror at the tragedy taking place high above their heads – until, of course, the Twin Towers came crashing down.

OPPOSITE & BELOW:

FIRST RESPONDERS

Heroic in their self-sacrifice and unstinting in their efforts, New York's firefighters became the face of 9/11. Hundreds were killed when the Twin Towers collapsed and their comrades worked frantically to save survivors from the wreckage. Many went on suffer long-term ill-effects from the inhalation of toxic smoke and dust, as well as from the sheer trauma of what they'd seen.

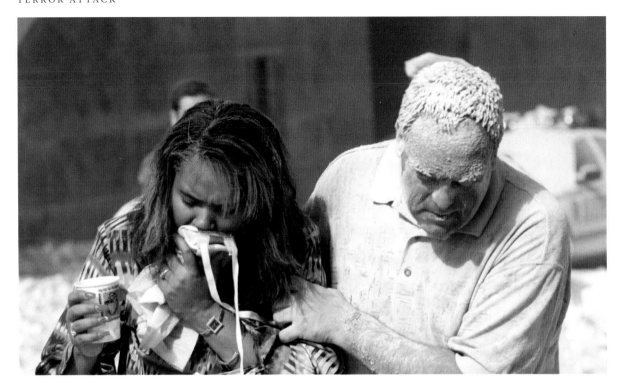

Even now, however, the scale of the atrocity had yet to become apparent. It had, it seemed, 'succeeded' beyond the terrorists' wildest dreams. The North Tower had been hit between the 93rd and 99th floors, which were now in flames; the South Tower had been hit between the 77th and 85th floors, causing another fire. By any normal standards, the casualties were grim.

ANNIHILATION

There was still no sign of panic, though. As officer workers filed down the emergency stairs of the two buildings on their way to safety, firefighters, paramedics and other rescuers passed them on their way up to the impacted areas. The atmosphere, while tense, was calm and orderly. At 9.59 a.m., however, the South Tower collapsed completely and without warning. Many hundreds were annihilated in its fall.

By 10.03, the terrorists' plan was out and news had reached the passengers of United Airlines Flight 93 from Newark to San Francisco, which had set out late before being hijacked. They decided they wouldn't simply sit and wait to die. Their attempt to storm the cockpit caused the hijackers to lose control and the airliner crashed in a field outside Stonycreek Township, Shanksville, PA.

BROUGHT LOW

At 10.28, an hour and 42 minutes after the initial impact, the North Tower collapsed in a cloud of smoke and dust. The Marriott Hotel, at its base, was obliterated by its fall. The sight was apocalyptic – but exemplary as well. The World Trade Center had been an iconic construction, representing the United States' global reach in finance and communications. The Pentagon was also a potent emblem of its military might.

Not that there was anything symbolic about the human cost. In all, 246 airline passengers and crew were killed, as well as 343 firefighters and paramedics and 60 police officers who'd joined in the rescue effort, along with over 2000 office workers. One business alone lost 700 staff, who left behind them 50 pregnant widows. More than 20,000 are believed to have been left injured.

OPPOSITE ABOVE:
WALKING WOUNDED
Dazed by the shock and struggling to breathe in the swirling clouds of often toxic dust, workers make their painful way to safety. The attacks had taken place at the very beginning of the working day: had they come later, the casualties could have been much higher.

OPPOSITE BELOW:
LURID LIGHT
15 September 2001 – four days on from the attack itself – the ruins of the World Trade Center were still burning.

OVERLEAF:
DUST AND ASHES
Although 21 people were found and pulled clear of the wreckage by search teams on the day following the disaster, no survivors were successfully rescued after that. Relief workers recovered 21,900 separate body parts thereafter. The devastation was a shocking sight, but the hidden effects were more insidious over the longer term: toxic dust caused an array of respiratory diseases and cancers.

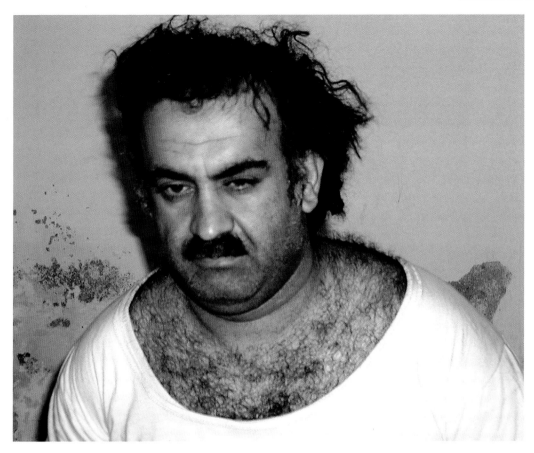

Nor were those affected all American. It had truly been a World Trade Center – the casualties included people from over 80 different countries.

A CRUEL CONSPIRACY

Eighteen hijackers had also died, although most people balked at including their names among the casualties and struggled to make sense of their cowardly cruelty. Young Arabs,

ABOVE:
KHALID SHAIKH MOHAMMED
Seen here after his capture in Rawalpindi, Pakistan, a year and a half after '9/11', KSM or Khalid Sheikh Mohammed eventually admitted to having masterminded the attack – along with several other atrocities.

OPPOSITE:
THE FACE OF EXHAUSTION
Firefighters at what was becoming known as 'Ground Zero' – the site of the Twin Towers – listen to an address by President George W. Bush three days after the attack.

they had acted under the direction of a hitherto-obscure organization: al-Qaeda. Literally meaning 'the Base', this had been formed by Arab veterans of the struggle against the Soviet occupation of Afghanistan. Under the leadership of Osama bin Laden, it aimed to create a 'caliphate' – an Islamic empire across the Muslim world.

Based in Sudan for several years, but expelled in 1996, its leaders had found refuge in Afghanistan – a country which, of course, they knew quite well. As wild in its anarchy as it was in its mountainous terrain, it could hardly have been further from Lower Manhattan – geographically, economically or culturally. The Taliban (literally 'Students' – they saw themselves as scholars of the Quran), who had taken over in the country in the decades since the Soviet defeat, shared many of al-Qaeda's extremist aims. They were backed by Afghanistan's eastern neighbour, Pakistan.

9/11 MEMORIAL POOL

One of the twin waterfall pools created to sit within the footprints of the original Twin Towers as a memorial to the 9/11 victims. Beside it stands the newly imagined World Trade Center complex, which is dominated by what is currently the tallest building in the Western Hemisphere.

OPERATION ENDURING FREEDOM

2001–2002

Great harm has been done to us,' President George W. Bush acknowledged during a joint address to the US Congress and the American nation on 20 September 2001. 'We have suffered great loss. And in our grief and anger we have found our mission and our moment. Freedom and fear are at war. The advance of human freedom – the great achievement of our time, and the great hope of every time – now depends on us. Our nation – this generation – will lift the dark threat of violence from our people and our future. We will rally the world to this cause by our efforts, by our courage. We will not tire, we will not falter and we will not fail.'

The strength of this commitment to the War on Terror was to be put to the test in the weeks and months that followed. Its strategic wisdom would be a question for the longer term. The president's words, although impassioned, were carefully chosen. He sought to speak both for the United States ('us', 'our nation') and the world at large ('human freedom'). 9/11 may have taken place on US soil, but it had, he said, been 'an attack on the heart and soul of the civilized world'. If the Taliban government didn't deliver Osama bin Ladcn and his al Qaeda comrades to US justice, it would face the fury of an outraged international community.

OPPOSITE:
TIME OUT
A sunny day in Tora Bora, 15 December 2001. A bomb blast plumes the sky with smoke but, unperturbed, an anti-Taliban militiaman takes a moment to trim his beard. War was becoming a way of life in Afghanistan.

LEFT:
MISSION READY
In October 2001, aboard the supercarrier USS *Carl Vinson* (CVN-70), the pilot of an F/A-18 Hornet completes an inspection of his plane prior to air strikes as part of Operation Enduring Freedom.

OPPOSITE:
DIRECTING OPERATIONS
President George W. Bush (centre) meets with cabinet officials on 10 October 2001. Beside him sit Secretary of State Colin Powell (left) and Defense Secretary Donald Rumsfeld (right).

BELOW:
SAFE HOME
An F-14 Tomcat about to touch down on the flight deck of the USS *Theodore Roosevelt* (CVN-71) after a sortie in support of Operation Enduring Freedom. The first priority of the military campaign was the destruction of al-Qaeda training camps and Taliban infrastructure in Afghanistan.

Worldwide support for the terrorists was negligible, but there was still suspicion of US motives. Since the Soviet Union's fall, America had stood unrivalled as a superpower, with the capacity to shape the world to its will. Granted, a terrible crime had been committed – and the Taliban's refusal to hand over bin Laden (there was, leader and founder Mullah Omar claimed, no evidence of his responsibility) appeared outrageous. But was it being seized on simply as a pretext for the imperialist projection of US power?

AN UNEQUAL STRUGGLE?

Afghanistan, by contrast, barely seemed a state at all – a country of chronic anarchy, stripped bare economically by decades of war. And yet, as it prepared to unleash the world's most powerful military force against a glorified gang of thugs armed with automatic rifles and handheld rocket launchers, the Bush administration still experienced considerable wariness.

The United States had learned all about the challenges of 'asymmetric warfare' in Vietnam. Afghanistan itself had been a graveyard for Soviet Russian might. Wild and undeveloped as the country was, it was a challenge for a military machine honed so carefully to tackle the most advanced of enemies that it seemed likely to struggle against a foe so lightly equipped and sketchily dug-in as the Taliban and their supporters. America's high-tech kit had been developed to do battle with a high-tech enemy; its super-sophisticated fighter jets and missile systems were geared to taking out appropriate targets.

NORTHERN ALLIANCE
A Northern Alliance soldier fires his gun down the street during street battles between Alliance troops and the Taliban in Kunduz on 26 November 2001.

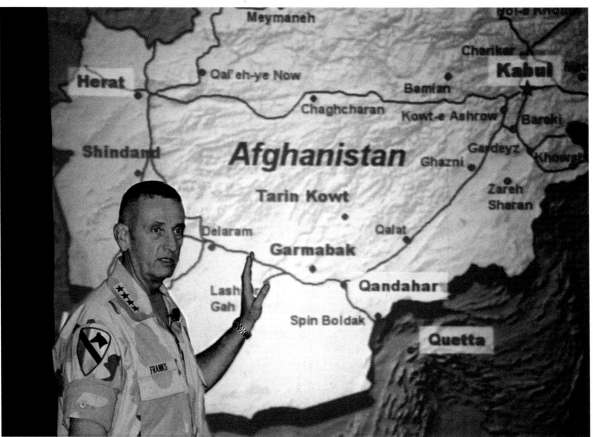

Beyond al-Qaeda training camps and a handful of Taliban targets, there was hardly anything in Afghanistan worth attacking.

CREATING A COALITION

In any case, before even the first shot was fired, there would be other asymmetries to address: those between the United States and its allies. In the developed world, these included long-established NATO partners Canada, the United Kingdom, Germany and France, along with members of the traditional 'Anglosphere' such as Australia and New Zealand.

Also to be considered were more recent NATO members from the former Soviet Bloc, from Albania to Poland. They were eager to establish their partnership with the Western powers as a going concern – as was Ukraine, which hoped one day to be allowed to join.

ISLAM VS ISLAMISM

The United States was also at pains to distinguish between Islam and Islamism – the latter a militant political creed – to avoid any war being seen as an attack on Muslims or their religion. Hence the importance

of bringing friendly Arab states – like the United Arab Emirates (UAE) – on board as well as reassuring the secular governments of countries with substantial Muslim populations: Turkey, for example, and Central Asian neighbours of Afghanistan such as Turkmenistan, Tajikistan and Uzbekistan.

SENSITIVITIES

Early plans to pursue retributory action under the initially named Operation Infinite Justice were quickly abandoned, as it seemed to carry religious overtones; terms such as 'crusade' were also set aside. The description 'Operation Enduring Freedom' reflected historic American ideals while also sounding neutral enough to appeal to other countries. (The word 'enduring' also reassured allies that this wasn't to be simply a vengeful lashing-out but a genuine bid to help construct a better world.)

All these countries came together under the auspices of the International Security Assistance Force (ISAF). While America committed 7000 troops, Britain 5700, France 4000 and Australia 1500, Azerbaijan sent 180 and Armenia some 130. All were welcome, every contribution

OPPOSITE ABOVE:
LONG WAY HOME
Another challenge Afghanistan posed to Western forces was its landlocked nature, at its closest almost 500km (300mi) from the sea. Carrier-based aircraft faced a considerable commute to and from the battle zone. This B-52H Stratofortress is returning from a 4500km (almost 3000-mi) bombing run from Diego Garcia, a British island-possession in the Indian Ocean.

OPPOSITE BELOW:
FRANKS DECLARATION
General Tommy Franks, Commander-in-Chief of US forces in Afghanistan, briefs reporters gathered in Tampa, Florida, in November 2001.

MY ENEMY'S ENEMY
Troops of General Daoud Khan's Northern Alliance soldiers regroup to prepare an attack on Kunduz. The allegiances and enmities at play in the unfolding conflict could be confusing.

helping drive home the message of international unanimity in opposition to al-Qaeda terror, including the UAE's three security guards and Ireland's seven headquarters staff. (Ireland also offered the use of Shannon Airport for transatlantic logistics flights; Turkmenistan, Uzbekistan and Tajikistan opened up their airspace to the Allies.)

AFGHAN ALLIES

Within Afghanistan itself, the so-called Northern Alliance had for years resisted the advance of the Taliban out of its original heartlands in the east and south, and therefore had a natural claim to be involved. It was barely even an 'alliance' in truth: a loose agglomeration of small militias led by local warlords of a type that had always abounded in Afghanistan.

It included Muhammad Mohaqiq with his (ethnically Hazara) Hezb-e Wahdat force; Atta Muhammad Nur's Tajik Jamiat-i Islami fighters and Abdul Rashid Dostum's Uzbek forces. Himself an Afghan of Uzbek ethnic background, Dostum is variously described as a 'general' and a 'warlord' – and in his time he has fully earned both descriptions. A conventional commander in the service of the Communist government in the Soviet era and then in the service of the West (ideologically, he travelled light), he was an old-fashioned tribal leader in between.

The Northern Alliance could be a formidable force collectively, but were often wayward when it came to following the Western line. The Bush administration did its best to tolerate this. It was important that Operation Enduring Freedom shouldn't seem to have been simply foisted on the Afghan people.

Afghanistan was not to be the only arena for Operation Enduring Freedom. There would be satellite actions from South America to Somalia, from the Sahara to the Philippines. It was widely reported that al-Qaeda was making common cause (or simply opportunistic arrangements) with local terrorist groups or criminal organizations. The United States was determined to curtail all these activities.

Nonetheless, wide as the scope of the war effort was, its primary focus remained on Afghanistan and, broad as the coalition was, it was very much led by the United States. It was American aircraft which, together with British support, got the fighting off to a thunderous start with a concerted campaign of bombing against al-Qaeda camps and Taliban positions.

OPPOSITE ABOVE:
MOUNTED SPECIAL FORCES
US Air Force Combat Controller Bart Decker makes his way across country on horseback with local guides and US Special Forces to help make ready a military airfield near the northern city of Mazar-i-Sharif. Western military officers found the rugged conditions awaiting them in Afghanistan decidedly alien – the utmost adaptability was required.

OPPOSITE BELOW:
ARMED AND READY
A US Special Forces soldier stands with fighters of the Northern Alliance in Zain-i-qala, near Mazar-i-Sharif, in readiness for a possible operation against a force of 2000 Taliban fighters.

A black-robed Taliban official with a rocket launcher looks on as foreign journalists are taken to view the scene of a US air strike that killed 11 at a clinic in Kandahar, south-eastern Afghanistan. However intense the military action, the fight for 'hearts and minds' was also constantly raging.

To begin with, moreover, the Bush administration's caution seemed exaggerated. The enemy had no answer to the sheer firepower Western forces could deploy. In a matter of weeks, the Taliban had been broadly dislodged from large areas of northern Afghanistan and had holed up in the city of Mazar-i-Sharif where they were joined by fleeing al-Qaeda fighters.

Mazar-i-Sharif had a sinister special place in Taliban mythology. When they'd taken the city in 1998, after weeks of increasingly bitter fighting, they had massacred up to 3000 of its captured defenders. The people here were Shi'ite Muslims – heretics and even infidels as far as the Sunni Muslims of the Taliban and al-Qaeda were concerned.

STRONGHOLD STORMED

Both sides expected some sort of heroic stand to be made at Mazar-i-Sharif, but that wasn't the case. The forces ranged against the city's defenders were just too strong, not so much in sheer firepower (although Taliban and al-Qaeda fighters were undoubtedly demoralized by aerial bombardments guided in by US Special Forces on the ground) as in the tireless persistence with which battle groups of the Northern Alliance kept advancing. And by the infallible ease with which – armed with advice

NEWS BRIEFING
Defense Secretary Donald Rumsfeld fields questions at a Pentagon press conference on 11 March 2002, to update the media on the progress of Operation Anaconda. Rumsfeld believed in decisive action and the use of overwhelming force in Afghanistan (and subsequently in Iraq). 'I don't do quagmires,' he maintained.

and intelligence from embedded CIA officers – they were able to find the weak points in the city's protective perimeter. The defenders were also softened up by 'psyops' (psychological operations) – propaganda leaflets being dropped for days in advance promising them their safety and a better life post-Taliban.

By the beginning of November, Muhammad Mohaqiq's Hezb-e Wahdat were advancing on the city from the north, while Atta Muhammad Nur's Jamiat-i Islami fighters were linking up with Abdul Rashid Dostum's forces south of the city. In the end it was to be Dostum who took the prize, sweeping into Mazar-i-Sharif with his men on 9 November. About a hundred fighters had been killed in the city's defence; some 500 were taken prisoner. Those who remained – a thousand or so – now broke and ran.

CITY CAPTURED

The loss of Mazar-i-Sharif brought the north of the country into the control of America's Afghan allies. More than this, it prompted a crisis of confidence among the Taliban. As the troops of the Northern Alliance now pushed south-east on the road to Kabul, they found opposition more or less melting away before them. And, on 13 November – only four days after taking Mazar-i-Sharif – they were able to walk into the Afghan capital, Kabul, unopposed.

Cutting their losses, the leaders of the Taliban and al-Qaeda had headed south, to the city of Kandahar: Afghan forces fought to root them out. Even as they did so, that December, battle was joined at Tora Bora in the south of the country, where al-Qaeda leaders had taken refuge in an elaborately fortified cave complex.

The creakiness of the coalition was underlined by the exception taken by the Northern Alliance to the arrival of two RAF Hercules heavy transport aircraft at Bagram Airbase, 60km (37mi) north of Kabul. Only with difficulty could they be persuaded that the British weren't setting out to establish a peacekeeping force and effectively take charge in an area the Afghan fighters regarded as emphatically their own.

Meanwhile, battle raged around the Tora Bora caves. A natural labyrinth of passages and bunkers, the complex had been used as a defensive stronghold for centuries. The caves were taken, but not before key al-Qaeda leaders, including Osama bin Laden, had escaped to Pakistan under the cover of almost a fortnight's fierce fighting.

OPERATION ANACONDA

March 2002 brought Operation Anaconda. The first major action to involve Western ground forces in direct engagement with the enemy, it was mounted against al-Qaeda and Taliban fighters. Beaten back from Tora Bora, they had gone to ground in isolated reaches of the Shah-i-Kot Valley and Arma Mountains. Some 30,000 troops – mostly American but also British, Australian, Canadian and even French and Spanish, as well as Afghan – rooted out around a thousand Islamist insurgents.

Operation Anaconda's climactic engagement came atop the mountain summit of Takur Ghar. Three US helicopter landings were beaten back by al-Qaeda fighters before the Americans gained the upper hand and pushed them out of the valley – but at the cost of seven men.

OPPOSITE:
TORA BORA FIGHT
A mujahedin keeps warm beside a fire at a captured al-Qaeda camp. Smoke rises behind him from an attack by US warplanes on a nearby al-Qaeda position in the Tora Bora region on 14 December 2001.

RIGHT:
TALIBAN UPRISING
CIA agent Johnny Michael Spann (right) and a US Special Forces soldier speak with a Northern Alliance commander in Mazar-i-Sharif. CIA agents were interrogating Taliban prisoners at the Qala-i-Jangi fortress in Mazar-i-Sharif when the prisoners staged an uprising and took over the makeshift prison on 25 November 2001, which led to hundreds being killed and many more wounded. Spann was killed by a Taliban prisoner who he was questioning.

BELOW:
BATTLE OF QALA-I-JANGI
American soldiers hide behind a barricade during an explosion, prior to fighting with Taliban forces at the fortress near Mazar-i-Sharif in November 2001.

LEFT & BELOW:
UPRISING
Northern Alliance fighters battle pro-Taliban forces at Mazar-i-Sharif on 27 November 2001. The Northern Alliance, helped by US and British special forces, quashed an uprising by captured Taliban fighters after a third day of heavy fighting around the fortress prison. The six-day uprising by Taliban and al-Qaeda prisoners resulted in hundreds dead. Of the more than 400 prisoners brought to the fortress, only 86 emerged alive.

UP IN SMOKE
British Royal Engineers from
Task Force Jacana destroy a
cave complex on the Pakistani
border between Paktika and
Paktia provinces as a follow-up
to Operation Anaconda.

RIGHT:
CAVE SEARCH
US soldiers prepare to storm
a cave to root out enemy
combatants believed to be holed
up in the wilds of the Shah-i-Kot
Valley in March 2002.

OPPOSITE:
ARTILLERY SUPPORT
Soldiers of the US Army's 10th
Mountain Division direct mortar
fire on to al-Qaeda and Taliban
positions in a far-flung corner
of Kapisa province in north-
eastern Afghanistan, as part of
Operation Anaconda.

It isn't only in armed strength that 'asymmetric warfare' is asymmetric. Western democracies typically find it harder to cope with casualties than insurgent enemies. Although the Taliban/al-Qaeda had lost anything up to 200 lives in the engagement, they understood how shocked US TV viewers would have been by the losses on their side. As with the Tet Offensive of 1968 in Vietnam, it wasn't enough for the West to win: public morale depended on overwhelming superiority. Therefore, over the weeks that followed, coalition forces carried on hunting the insurgents in their hiding places. Al-Qaeda were going to remain a threat for as long as they continued to have support in Afghanistan. And they were going to have that for as long as the Taliban had any sort of foothold there.

OPPOSITE:
OPERATION PTARMIGAN, APRIL 2002
A British Royal Marine sits behind his machine gun during a mopping-up operation in Ginger Valley, south-eastern Afghanistan. Although their government had been quickly toppled, the Taliban remained a threatening presence in remoter regions.

BELOW:
AFGHAN GUARD
An Afghan soldier guards the war-ravaged former royal palace of Darul Aman in Kabul, then the battalion headquarters of the Afghan National Army.

RIGHT:
SOUND OF FREEDOM
Young Afghans in a Kabul marketplace make the most of their liberation by listening to music in November 2001. Taliban oppression had extended far beyond what Westerners might have seen as religious and political spheres into practically every area of daily life.

BELOW:
BAREFACED LIBERTY
High spirits reign in a Kabul barbershop as 23-year-old Jawaid has his beard shaved off. The Taliban had required that every adult male grow enough facial hair to be grabbed in the hand – but not all men could manage this. Jawaid had been arrested three times for hair-based violations.

CELEBRATION
A group of boys exult at the sight of US planes pounding Taliban positions above the Shomali Plain, just north of Kabul, on 29 October 2001. It would be untrue to claim that the Taliban had enjoyed no support across Afghanistan, but in much of the country their rule had been resented.

RECONSTRUCTION

As 2002 began, Afghanistan's 'freedom' had arguably been secured. How 'enduring' it was going to be was much less clear, however. Taliban rule might be a fast-receding memory and many of its leaders might have slipped across the border into Pakistan; but activists and fighters remained throughout the remoter countryside.

'Mopping-up' operations were to continue well into the spring – months after Hamid Karzai's Interim Administration had supposedly taken power after the fall of the Taliban. Karzai's government was based on a compromise thrashed out at talks held in Bonn, Germany, at the beginning of December 2001. Together with international politicians and officials – not only from the United States but from other countries in the region, including Russia, Iran, Pakistan and India – representatives of the Northern Alliance and other important Afghan groupings had gathered. The anti-Taliban opposition in Afghanistan had organized itself largely along ethnic lines, as we've seen, but the northern Tajiks and the southern Pashtun were most strongly represented at the German conference.

OPPOSITE:
COLLATERAL DAMAGE
Afghanistan had been saved – yet it had been all but destroyed in the process. Not only its physical infrastructure, but its institutions and its social order had to be rebuilt.

LEFT:
HONOURED GUEST
US President George W. Bush (right) receives Hamid Karzai in the Oval Office on 28 January 2002. Washington invested a considerable amount of geopolitical capital in the new Afghan leader.

OPPOSITE:
UNCOVERED
The suggestion that this had been a war for women's rights was regarded with some cynicism. Nevertheless, Afghan girls were now allowed to uncover their faces in public and go to school.

BELOW:
MUTUAL ADVANTAGE
'Photo-opportunities' with chairman Hamid Karzai (right) enabled Western leaders like UK Prime Minister Tony Blair (left) to present themselves as major movers and shakers, while also shoring up the Interim Administration's authority at home.

Karzai was conspicuous by his absence, in fact: the Pashtun leader was still organizing resistance to the Taliban around Kandahar. He was well-known to the international community, however. In the months before 9/11 he had spent time in North America and Europe trying to lobby support for Western intervention in the country. After the attacks, his task had become a great deal easier.

Now he had to lead a civil administration that could command respect, both within the country and beyond its borders, pending proper elections the following year. As important as US patronage was for him, it brought with it the suspicion among many of his countrymen – and commentators elsewhere in the world – that he was actually an agent of the CIA.

'FRIENDLY FIRE'

That US support could be a mixed blessing to an Afghan leader was underlined dramatically on 5 December. The Bonn Conference had only just appointed him Chairman of the Interim Administration when his Kandahar headquarters was hit by a misdirected air strike called down by his US protectors. Several of his staff were killed, although Karzai survived, with minor injuries.

It's tempting to treat this incident as a metaphor for Afghanistan, a country ravaged by its supposed saviours in the preceding months. And certainly, the costs of the war were to be seen all around, wherever you went, in everything from bomb-craters and blast-damaged buildings to maimed children. Somewhere in the region of 2000 civilians were listed killed or missing; between 8000 and 12,000 Afghan fighters for the Taliban had died along with an unknown number of Northern Alliance supporters.

Afghanistan's trauma was only intensified by the sense that there had been wheels within wheels – an ethnic conflict within the political one. The predominantly Tajik Northern Alliance had allegedly committed mass-rape and murder as it made its way through the Pashtun regions of the country.

Not, of course, that loss or anguish were anything particularly new for Afghanistan. This had been only the latest in a succession of bloody wars. Besides, the Taliban had arguably damaged the country much more deeply with their religious fanaticism and their prohibitions on music, the arts, most social activities and sport.

OPPOSITE ABOVE:
PITIABLE PLIGHT
A maimed boy begging in Kabul in February 2002 illustrates two pressing problems for Afghanistan: the legacy of war in injuries, disabilities and bereavements; and the desperate economic straits that had made child labour more or less the norm.

OPPOSITE BELOW:
WRECKAGE
Amid the ruins in January 2002, an Ariana Afghan Airlines plane at Kabul Airport offers a link with a world beyond. Was Afghanistan as a whole ready for take-off?

OVERLEAF:
READY TO REBUILD
Workers take freshly fired bricks from a Kabul kiln in July 2002. Already battered by years of conflict, Afghanistan's cities and towns had taken a further hammering from coalition forces during Operation Enduring Freedom. Much of the reconstruction required was of the most basic and physical nature.

Under Taliban rule, girls and women had been harshly oppressed; they were barred from the worlds of work and education and forced to go covered from head to foot in public, wearing burkhas. Adultery had been punishable by public flogging – and extremely broadly defined, it included women simply being seen out in public with unrelated males.

In the same spirit of puritanism, the Taliban had initially suppressed the country's cultivation of opium poppies. By 1999, however, they'd felt compelled to encourage it to avoid economic collapse. Money markets care little whether a society they are dealing with is repressive or enlightened. So preposterously exacting were the Taliban's strictures, however, that the Afghan economy could barely function.

Governments in the developing world are entitled to be cautious in their dealings with foreign companies, whose motives are seldom altruistic. Yet it's one thing to guard against neocolonial exploitation; quite another to inaugurate a tax regime so draconian it seems deliberately designed to keep the outer world at bay. Afghanistan had been in ruins, therefore, not only in terms of its infrastructure, but also psychologically and economically before the latest round of conflict had begun.

JOB DONE
Defense Secretary Donald Rumsfeld visits US Special Forces troops in Kabul on 1 May 2003 – the day that he announced an end to 'major combat' in the country.

STEPPING UP

An Afghan soldier poses on
a Russian-built T62 tank at
the Army Training Centre in
Kabul. By the middle of 2003,
with most of the country
comparatively stable and
'permissive' for government
forces, the Americans were
eager to step back and take a
secondary role.

When Hamid Karzai was sworn in as leader of the Interim Administration on 22 December 2001, he faced some daunting challenges. The first was to attain for his administration the overarching authority that would allow it to at least hope to establish order countrywide. With this in mind, he chose as members of his 30-strong cabinet representatives of Afghanistan's four principal ethnic groups. Pashtuns and Tajiks predominated, but there were also Uzbeks and Hazara. However, if there were ethnic rivalries and resentments to be assuaged, there were also individual egos to be appeased. Major warlords were carefully brought into his big tent.

INSTABILITY CONTINUES

It was an encouraging start; for now at least, the Afghan Interim Administration had an aspirational air. However, there was nowhere, realistically, for its writ to run. Kabul and other major urban centres might have fallen comparatively easily, but that did not mean the country as a whole had been pacified. Outside of the cities, the situation remained unstable and the roads unsafe.

ABOVE:
DEFENDING THE HOMELAND
A group of Afghan soldiers practise shooting. It was important that in the longer term responsibility for the country's security should rest with the Afghan National Army; however, its training was conducted by officers from the ISAF (International Security Assistance Force).

OPPOSITE:
ON GUARD
Afghan National Army troops stand guard at an emplacement by Kabul's Intercontinental Hotel in December 2003, providing security as delegates prepare to ratify a new constitution. Despite the end of 'major combat', Afghanistan effectively remained on a wartime footing for months and even years.

OVERLEAF:
NATO DEPLOYMENT
A German soldier, part of the UN-mandated International Security Assistance Force, sits in a jeep with his rifle in his hands during a military patrol in the fourth police district in Kabul, August 2003.

OPPOSITE ABOVE:
WEAPONS CACHE
Rifles at the ready, US soldiers make their way into a cave in the Adi Ghar Mountains near Kandahar in southern Afghanistan, in search of a Taliban weapons cache they believe may be inside.

OPPOSITE BELOW:
SEARCH AND DESTROY
A US soldier searches in a well for stored weapons. The departing Taliban had left caches of weapons and supplies behind them to speed their retreat – and facilitate their potential return once things settled down. The Americans made it a priority to find and neutralize these stores.

On 17 April 2002, in a speech at the Virginia Military Institute, President George W. Bush announced a major package of assistance to help Afghanistan. It would, he claimed, recall the work of Secretary of State George C. Marshall, whose 'Marshall Plan' financed reconstruction in Europe after World War II. (This promise wasn't quite to be fulfilled: the $38 billion America and its allies found for Afghanistan over the next six years may sound like an enormous sum but it didn't go far in restoring an economy in ruins.)

RESTLESS RESCUERS

Meanwhile, with the war still not yet really won and Hamid Karzai and his colleagues confined to Kabul, Afghanistan's Western deliverers were itching to be gone. They feared that public attitudes to the continuing conflict might be shifting in their respective countries. In the immediate aftermath of the 9/11 attacks, it had seemed self-evident that 'something must be done' to tackle terrorism, and action against the Taliban and al-Qaeda in Afghanistan had won strong support. Gradually, however, that initial shock had been subsiding.

That the coalition had enjoyed such early successes had undoubtedly been good news, but the need for a longer-term engagement was starting to be questioned. Military analysts and experts were astonished – to say the least – when, as early as July 2002, Donald Rumsfeld announced that the war was over. Little had changed by May 2003, when he declared that 'major combat' had been completed, but the Defense Secretary was making a shrewd assessment of what he thought Americans would stand.

PUBLIC PATIENCE

If the hostilities hadn't yet come to an end, public patience was perhaps approaching one. By comparison with those of the Taliban, American casualties had been laughably small: 12 soldiers and a single CIA officer had been killed. However, every one of their deaths had been widely reported in the media and taken extremely seriously by newspaper readers and TV viewers who wanted to be certain that their compatriots' sacrifices hadn't been in vain.

That March, moreover, another US-led coalition had invaded Iraq, where Saddam Hussein's regime was seen as threatening the peace of the Middle East and the wider world. Where, Americans began to wonder, would it all end?

STARTING FROM SCRATCH
Captain Bill Mandrick of the US Army (right) stands amid the ruins of Kunduz's teacher training college on 8 June 2002, as local workers clear the site for reconstruction. The reconstruction programme was a great opportunity for Afghanistan to start afresh, but there was no mistaking the scale of the challenge the country faced.

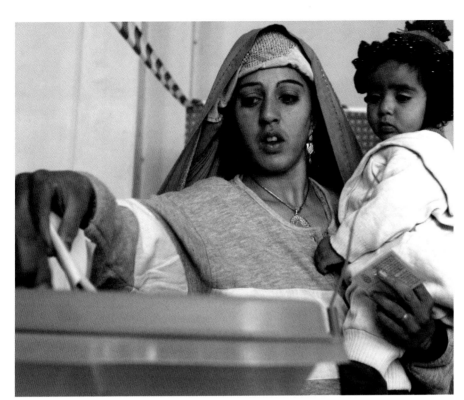

OPPOSITE:
ON THE STUMP
Last seen liberating Mazar-i-Sharif, Abdul Rashid Dostum followed what became a familiar path for Afghan warlords from the field of battle into the political arena. Running for the presidency in 2004, he lost to the liberal Ashraf Ghani, but was appointed vice president.

LEFT:
A VOICE IN THE FUTURE
A woman casts her vote for president during Afghanistan's first direct democratic election in October 2004. Might her child grow up in a land of genuinely 'enduring freedom'?

BELOW:
PEOPLE POWER
Workers form a human chain to transport ballot boxes to a counting centre during the election. Over three-quarters of the Afghan electorate turned out to vote in the historic election almost three years after the Taliban regime fell.

This wasn't the only reason the Americans wanted to take a background role. Afghan sovereignty and democracy were at stake. (Hence Hamid Karzai's confirmation as his country's president at this time.) But, given the destruction caused by the recent war and the continuing gravity of the situation, politically and economically, a more gradual handover of management might have been expected.

As an interim measure, efforts were made for front-line US troops to be replaced by soldiers from the other ISAF (International Security Assistance Force) countries while the Americans withdrew into the background. In August 2003, control of ISAF passed officially to NATO. Increasingly, Westerners were, as far as practicable, removed from active combat duty and steered into advisory and training roles with the Afghan National Army – newly re-established – as well as policing duties and relief work. Again, while offering respect for the autonomy of the Afghan people, the decision was made with the reactions of the media at home in mind.

Normalization was the order of the day. By October 2004 Afghanistan would be able to have its first presidential election. Was a brighter future now in store?

American forces remained in Afghanistan, but very much behind the scenes and largely confined to Bagram Airbase in Parwan, north of Kabul. However, they remained a potential target for insurgents and rigorous security disciplines were still needed.

VEHICLE CHECK
A US Marine from 6th Marine Regiment, 2nd Marine Division uses a mirror to inspect the undercarriage of an Afghani commercial truck delivering pre-fabricated concrete bunker walls to Camp Stonewall at Bagram Airbase in Parvan province.

LINGERING INSURGENCY

As 2005 started, President Hamid Karzai presided over a brave new Afghanistan: free, democratic and forward-looking in its attitudes, if badly damaged by years of war. Much had been achieved. An oppressive regime of religious fanatics had been removed. Also, a major blow had been dealt to the terrorists they had harboured under their protection – a group responsible for one of the most terrible atrocities of recent history.

With Western assistance, a huge programme of reconstruction was underway to rebuild the country and develop new amenities and institutions that were more appropriate to the first decade of the 21st century.

That said, the ointment was not short of flies. Defense Secretary Donald Rumsfeld might have been justified in claiming that major hostilities had concluded some time earlier, but by now the 'mopping up' had lasted longer than the war. The new order was to some extent illusory – the ruling elite still more or less corralled in Kabul and large areas of the provinces still too unsafe to venture into.

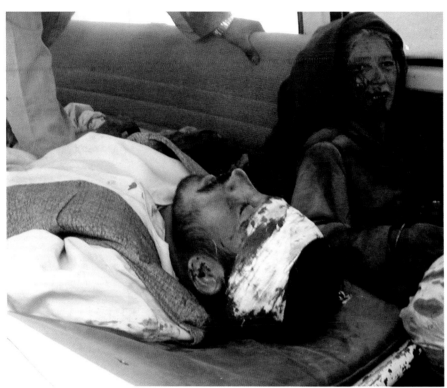

LEFT:
STILL SUFFERING
Two bomb-blast victims are carried in an ambulance near the Spin Boldak border post, southeast of Kandahar in October 2005. As insurgents continued their long, slow war of attrition along the Pakistani border, it was left to ordinary civilians to pay the price.

OPPOSITE:
DOCTOR'S ROUNDS
A US Navy medic on patrol looking out for cases of illness and disease in a street in Mihtarlam in eastern Afghanistan, March 2005. Providing healthcare could help win 'hearts and minds'.

BELOW:
FLAMES OF FUTILITY
An Afghan policeman in Jalalabad surveys the burning wreck of a car blown up by a suspected suicide bomber some 300m (980ft) from the governor's mansion in the eastern city.

Few felt inclined to question the situation too closely, however. The US president and his political colleagues (even those in opposition) owed their status to the new arrangement, however unsatisfactory, while America and its Western allies preferred to see the successes than scrutinize the shortcomings. Yet as the months went by and the Afghan government failed to convincingly consolidate its hold on the country as a whole, it seemed appropriate to wonder when the much-anticipated future of peace and prosperity was going to begin.

UNFINISHED BUSINESS

Moreover, when would the supporters of the old regime – though soundly beaten in battle three years before, brought down from government, expelled from Kabul and dispersed through the countryside – be definitively defeated? For even now there was no sign of this. The Taliban seemed to have passed seamlessly from tyrannical government to terrorist insurgents. While the government in Kabul was seemingly secure, the guerrilla war in the countryside – low intensity but

OPPOSITE ABOVE:
SUICIDE BOMB
Police investigate the scene of a suicide attack in Kabul, September 2006. In addition to the bomber, one British soldier and four civilians were killed. As with the 9/11 attacks, suicide bombings weaponized the idealistic spirit of self-sacrifice, but were cruel in the indiscriminate carnage that they caused.

OPPOSITE BELOW:
WHO'S IN CONTROL?
An Afghan policeman covers his face as he keeps watch at a suicide blast site in October 2006. The second half of 2006 saw a spate of suicide bombings in Afghanistan. This one, in Kabul, wounded at least three people. From a strictly military point of view, such attacks were fairly pointless – but they undermined the claims of the authorities to be in control.

dismally persistent – was taking a horrendous daily toll. Local officials, law enforcement officers, foreign aid workers, bus and lorry drivers – and, of course, ordinary villagers – found themselves persecuted by the insurgents' campaign of terror.

The reality should have been so different. The Afghan National Army massively outnumbered its Taliban adversaries: 350,000-odd to 50–60,000. It was overwhelmingly superior in firepower, too, having been equipped and trained by its Western sponsors – who still supplied advice, intelligence and air support. The outcome, on the face of it, was not in doubt.

REBEL RESILIENCE

As we've seen, however, the guerrillas' weakness could be a source of strength. Without big armies in the field, they couldn't hope to take Kabul or Kandahar or conquer major tranches of territory, but then they couldn't realistically be bombarded from the air or cut off logistically on the ground. They didn't have sophisticated command centres, advanced air defence systems to be knocked out in missile strikes or an air force that could be grounded by a bombing raid. For heavy artillery they had hand-held rocket launchers; for a communications infrastructure satellite or mobile phones. They travelled light, taking food from villagers and finding water as they went.

OVERLEAF:
VOTE OF CONFIDENCE
Women in Kabul queue up in September 2005 to cast their votes in the nation's first parliamentary elections since 1988. All but imprisoned in their homes during the Taliban era, Afghan women had a great deal at stake in the development of democracy in their country.

SEARCH AND DESTROY MISSIONS

CH-47 Chinook helicopters descend on a remote landing zone in Landi Khel, north-eastern Afghanistan, to pick up US soldiers who have been trying to find a weapons cache. In a country more than three times the size of Britain – and highly mountainous over much of that area – these were invariably frustrating and often fruitless searches.

ABOVE:
WELCOME OUTSTAYED?
While the West's role in freeing Afghans from the Taliban had been appreciated, their continuing presence created mounting friction. Five Afghans were killed when a US military truck hit a car in Kabul on 29 May 2006; nine more would die, with 60 wounded, in the riots that followed.

OPPOSITE:
ISLAMIC IRE
Visually depicting Islam's Prophet is regarded as an act of sacrilege by many believers. Afghan protesters shared the anger of their coreligionists around the world when, in February 2006, the Danish government refused to act against a magazine that had published cartoons in which Muhammad had been represented.

As time went on, the Taliban insurgents grew emboldened. They may not have been winning as such, but they weren't being quashed either, and in their calculation this was a triumph of sorts. Their defeat in 2001 had undoubtedly struck a body blow. Many fighters had slipped across the Pakistan border to lie low in the mountains on that side.

Nonetheless, their camps had become larger and more permanent and their function had slowly shifted. Initially pitched as hideouts by men in headlong flight, they had become bases for a force that was actively regrouping. (With, some analysts suspected, the secret support of the Pakistani authorities, although officially they were hunting these fighters down.) Soon, they were starting to slip back into Afghanistan again, rested and restored in spirit, augmented in numbers and comprehensively re-armed.

MORALE MALAISE

Conversely, in the Afghan National Army (ANA) morale was ebbing. Corruption was rife. Costly equipment, weapons, ammunition and provisions disappeared before they could reach the troops; foreign aid evaporated while soldiers went unpaid. Inevitably, perhaps. Hamid Karzai's whole approach in choosing his government had been to reward all those he saw as having supported his struggle with the Taliban or to offer favours to those whose cooperation he saw himself as needing in the months to come. What alternative did he have – it might reasonably be asked – in the absence of any viable pre-existing structures and with the need to turn a free-for-all into a state?

Understandable or not, it meant that bribery and fraud were intrinsic to the institutional structure of the ANA, which meant that cynicism and apathy were intrinsic to it too. It didn't help that, while ANA recruiters were admirably thorough in bringing in representatives of all Afghanistan's main ethnic groups, they tended to bring their rivalries and resentments with them. And, more alarmingly,

ROYAL MARINE INSERTION
With its rotors turning, an RAF CH-47 Chinook waits while members of A Company, 2nd Battalion, Royal Regiment of Fusiliers board via the helicopter's rear loading ramp. To the right, newly arrived at Now Zad, Helmland province, during Operation Silica, are K Company of 42 Commando, Royal Marines.

ABOVE:
MANGLED MACHINERY
Charred and twisted, the remains of a US Army Humvee
spoil the desert view in July 2006. Not since Vietnam had
the American military machine been brought so low.

OPPOSITE ABOVE:
OPERATION RED WINGS
US Navy SEALs assisted in actions against the insurgency,
bringing their expertise to bear in situations where the
Afghan National Army couldn't cope. And they still risked
their lives. Of these participants in Operation Red Wings
– an attack up eastern Afghanistan's Korengal Valley in
June–July 2005 – all except Petty Officer 2nd Class Marcus
Luttrell (third from right) were killed.

OPPOSITE BELOW:
DEMOCRATIC DAWN
An election worker awaits the first arrivals at Kabul's
Eid-Gah mosque, a polling station for the Parliamentary
Election in September 2005.

their loyalties. The idea of an Afghan nation-
state to which they owed their ultimate
allegiance was new, unfamiliar – and, frankly,
uncompelling. Soldiers signed up to take their
pay from the state and, up to a point, to serve it,
but their first attachments were to their home
communities and their ethnic groups.

OPERATION RED WINGS

If the Taliban couldn't take back power,
then, the Afghan government couldn't quite
enforce its authority, despite the assistance
of its Western allies. Operation Red Wings, a
bid by US forces to take back the initiative in
the country's Korengal Valley in the summer
of 2005, ended up having the opposite effect.
Technically, Western power prevailed, but the
US victory proved pyrrhic, coming at the
cost of 19 lives. Moreover, a downed Chinook
was an important propaganda coup for the
insurgents and a feather in the cap of military
commander Ahmad Shah. He was already
emerging as a charismatic leader of the pro-
Taliban insurgents in the north-east. As recently
as 2001, Shah had fought against the Islamists.

MOUNTING COST
Donald Rumsfeld's successor as Defense Secretary, Robert Gates, visits US troops in January 2007. While this trip, so early in his tenure, underlined America's continuing commitment to Afghanistan, his comments made clear that he shared Rumsfeld's resolve to see US involvement scaled down with all manageable speed.

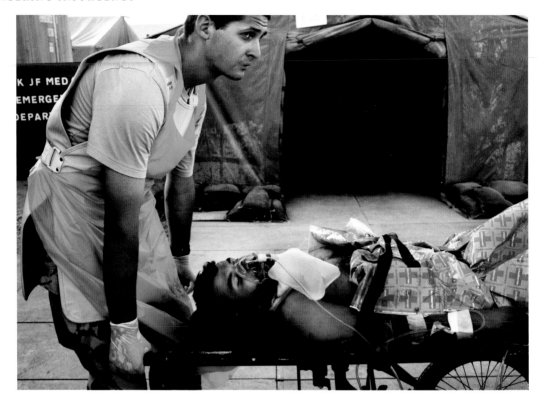

His rise is a reminder that the Afghan fighters didn't just travel light in arms and supplies, but in ideology. Local loyalties – and immediate advantage – mattered more.

So it had always been since ancient times in one of the world's most persistently violent and anarchic countries. These, however, definitely weren't ancient times. With Afghanistan getting too hot for them after the humiliation they'd dealt the Americans, Shah and his comrades took time out in Pakistan. Yet, the video they'd taken of their ambush was fighting for them now. 'Going viral' around the world, it was taken up exultantly by the insurgents' growing army of online cyber-supporters.

VIRTUAL DIMENSION

As with 9/11, a real event had taken place: people had died and there had been real consequences. The wider insurgency had been taking a very real and heavy toll on the people of Afghanistan too. At the same time, the conflict had an important virtual dimension. In London, Leicester, Dearborn and Toronto,

ALL PHOTOGRAPHS:
CASUALTIES OF WAR
Afghan police manning a road block, a passing patrol of ISAF soldiers, NGO relief workers unloading a consignment of supplies – all were targets for the insurgents at this time. Civilian women out shopping or children walking to school were acceptable as collateral damage. Keep up a 'low-intensity' conflict long enough and it cumulatively becomes a catastrophe.

And the Afghan insurgency was gathering momentum. Where 2005 had seen 27 suicide bombings, 2006 saw five times that number (139); the number of attacks by remote-controlled IED (improvised explosive device) would more than double. Both sides had to bear responsibility.

In their eagerness to spare their ground troops, the Americans relied more on air power. One air strike in July 2007 in Nangrahar claimed 49 lives – 37 of them women and children, and all thought to be civilians. The following day, a suicide bombing in Kabul killed 41 and wounded 130 – again, all civilians. The trauma to victims and communities apart, the treatment of the injured placed an extra burden on already hard-pressed hospitals.

exultant young men (and a few young women) were watching this footage on their phones, seeing strong, determined Muslims hitting back at the *Kafir* (non-believing) USA.

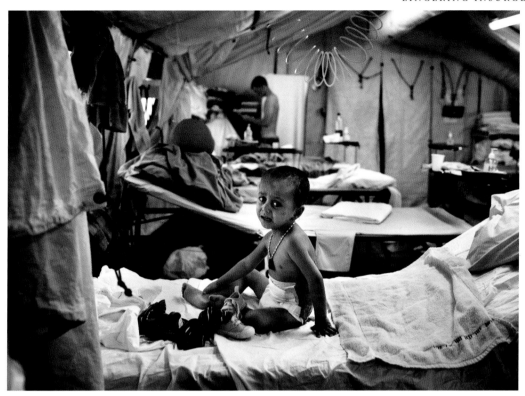

LEFT:
SUPPLY DROP
Paratroopers watch as bundles
carrying food and water are
dropped in Paktika province in
October 2007. Rugged terrain,
remote locations and dangerous
conditions along scarce roads
made it easier to keep US troops
supplied by air.

OVERLEAF:
HELPING HAND
Soldiers of the Kalagush
Provincial Reconstruction
Team traverse a rocky mountain
pass en route to an isolated
village in eastern Afghanistan
in June 2007. Such units
worked with communities,
assisting in everything from
health provision to engineering
projects as a way of winning
'hearts and minds'.

CLEARING THE WAY
Soldiers from Bravo Company, 2-508th Parachute Infantry Regiment, search a mountain for Taliban members and weapons near Waghez, Ghazi province, in September 2007.

The situation only worsened and it was with mounting alarm that Robert Gates, now US Defense Secretary, took NATO allies to task in 2007 for not sending more soldiers: 'We risk allowing what has been achieved in Afghanistan to slip away.' Armad Shah was killed in a clash with Pakistani soldiers in April 2008, but the insurgency as a whole was only moving up a gear. Taliban attacks that year were up 40 per cent on the number in 2007, which had already been alarming.

COLLATERAL DAMAGE

That collateral killings were up as well only added to the sense of a situation spiralling out of control. Between January and July 2008, 119 civilians died in US air strikes. One strike alone in August, when a US plane fired on civilians at Azizabad in Herat province, killed up to 60 adults and 30 children. Operation Enduring Freedom had not been intended to include the slaughter of civilians: its moral authority was hanging by a thread.

ABOVE:
KILLED IN ACTION
23 October 2007: US soldiers carry a fallen comrade up the Abascar Ridge towards a waiting medevac helicopter. Sergeant Larry Rougle, of West Valley City, Utah, on his third tour of duty in Afghanistan, was killed by small-arms fire during a battle with insurgents.

OPPOSITE ABOVE:
UNDER FIRE
US soldiers and Afghan workers lie low in a bunker at their forward operating base in the Korengal Valley under sustained – and increasingly accurate – mortar fire. Generally by this time – October 2007 – ISAF forces were feeling like sitting ducks, although the situation was at its gravest in the east. Kunar province's Korengal was nicknamed 'the Valley of Death'.

OPPOSITE BELOW:
MILITARY MISADVENTURES
The hazards of war can be unexpected. These Afghan soldiers are being treated at the aid station of a US base in the Pech River Valley. They sustained their injuries while driving with night-vision goggles on a mission with US forces and ended up going over a cliff edge.

OVERLEAF:
AT EASE
Two Grenadier Guardsmen relax next to a personalized Union Jack flag at the Delhi Patrol Base, South Helmand, in 2007. All British combat operations in Afghanistan between 2002 and 2014 came under the overall codename of 'Operation Herrick'.

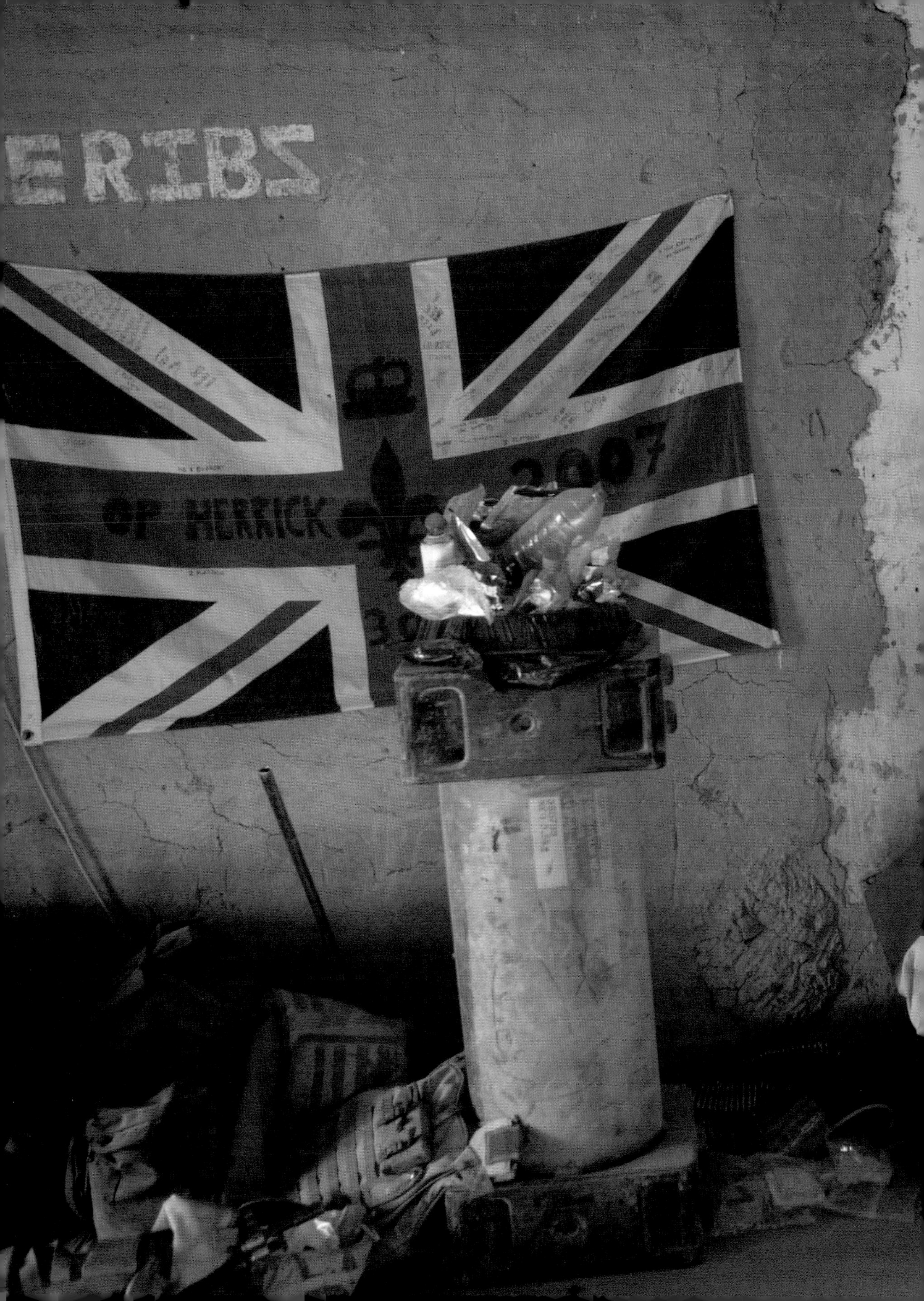
ERIBS
OP HERRICK
2007

ALL PHOTOGRAPHS:
IN A MOMENT
A British paratrooper stumbles and recovers (opposite and left) while his comrade fires through an opening in the compound wall (below). The empty cartridges from his rifle can be seen flying through the air. Operation Oqab Tsuka (Eagle's Summit) brought an important victory over the Taliban in 2008.

PRINCE OF WAR
Prince Harry passes a local as he patrols the town of Garmsir in Helmand in January 2008. Then third in line to the throne, the prince served two tours in Afghanistan with the British Army.

SURGING FORWARD?

Barack Obama had told excited Americans on the presidential campaign trail through the summer of 2008: 'Yes, we can!' He at least could, it became clear, when he won the presidency later that year. An African-American president would have been unthinkable just a generation earlier. Yet, here he was.

Not surprisingly, optimism was to be Obama's hallmark emotion. The road to peace and justice might be steep, he acknowledged in his election victory speech, but 'I have never been more hopeful than I am tonight'. The upbeat feeling went round the world – but would it make a stop at Afghanistan – the place where good intentions came to die?

As a senator, Obama had opposed the invasion of Iraq, believing it could only create a damaging distraction. America and its allies had to focus on 'the right war' – Afghanistan – he argued. He certainly had a case. The prospect of the insurgency finally being crushed appeared, if anything, to be receding. If a British-led force had scored a significant victory at Musa Qala, Helmand, at the end of 2007, forcing the Taliban into a humiliating retreat, they'd restored the balance – and then some – six months later.

OPPOSITE:
ON PATROL
US Marines with 3rd Battalion, 6th Marine Regiment, investigate a possible improvised explosive device (IED) while on a patrol during their deployment in 2010.

LEFT:
SURPRISE
US soldiers of the 10th Mountain Division explore a possible ambush on an insurgent position in the Onkai Valley, May 2009. The light infantry division had come to eastern Afghanistan's Wardak province that January, as part of the first contingent of the 'surge'.

OPPOSITE:
A NARROW ESCAPE
A US Marine sprints for safety as an IED (improvised explosive device) goes up behind him in Garmsir, Helmand province, July 2009. IEDs accounted for almost half of Western casualties that year.

BELOW:
OVERWATCH DUTIES
The 10th Mountain Division occupies an appropriately elevated position in this observation post on a summit above the Tangi Valley in Wardak province, May 2009.

In June 2008, insurgents had stormed the prison in Kandahar, freeing 1200 prisoners, 400 of them Taliban. The news a few months afterwards that the Taliban and al-Qaeda had parted company was welcome – but did nothing to end the conflict.

ONWARDS NOT UPWARDS

George W. Bush had come to the conclusion that US involvement in Afghanistan would either have to be scaled up radically or effectively abandoned. The 68,000 troops he already had in Afghanistan hadn't made a breakthrough. As long as the Afghan government and its Western supporters weren't obviously winning, they were losing.

Lives were being lost, while resources were depleted and political capital slowly drained away. Yet public resistance was growing. Understandably in the circumstances, while minded to send more troops to take the fight to the Taliban, Bush let the final decision pass to his successor.

SEIZING THE INITIATIVE

A newly elected president, Obama had the political credit to take the decision to step up involvement in Afghanistan. (And, perhaps, a need to, given the right-wing smears casting doubt on the patriotism of America's first Black President.) On 11 December 2009, while addressing cadets of the United States Military Academy at West Point, New York – and being watched by TV viewers nationwide – he announced what would popularly be referred to as the 'surge'.

'As Commander-in-Chief,' he said, 'I have determined that it is in our vital national interest to send an additional 30,000 US troops to Afghanistan.' An injection of fresh strength into a flagging military effort, they would allow the West to 'seize the initiative' immediately, while in the slightly longer term helping to build an Afghan state with the capacity to move forward on its own.

The surge would be strictly temporary. In 18 months, he said, American troops would be able to start coming home. Obama was insistent on that point. Committed as he was to the war in Afghanistan, he was as conscious as former Defense Secretary Donald Rumsfeld had been that public patience wasn't going to be everlasting. And by now, of course, six years had passed since Rumsfeld had pronounced all 'major combat' over.

OPPOSITE ABOVE:
DRONE DEMONSTRATION
Islamic fundamentalists in Peshawar protest US drone attacks on insurgent camps in Pakistan in April 2009. They had a point. That year, 54 US drone strikes killed over 380 militants, but also at least 70 civilians.

OPPOSITE BELOW:
ON THE MOVE
Weapons at the ready, Royal Marines commandos cross an open area in Helmand province in Jackal armoured patrol vehicles during Operation Fibonacci, February 2009.

STRATEGY REVIEW
President Barack Obama and his advisors hold a strategy review on Afghanistan in the Situation Room of the White House in September 2009.

The attempt to scale down the involvement of US and ISAF (International Security Assistance) forces had foundered on the fact that the Afghan National Army quite simply wasn't up to the job. Air strikes allowed the Americans a more 'arm's length' engagement with the enemy. As we've seen, however, they weren't effective against lightly armed, loosely formed insurgent groups operating in open country; and, of course, they had produced alarming collateral casualties.

ABOVE:
COMBAT OUTPOST KEATING
A view over Combat Outpost Keating, a small US military outpost on the Pakistan-Afghanistan border in Nuristan province. The base was nearly overrun following an attack on 3 October 2009, when eight Americans and four Afghan defenders were killed. A few days later the base was abandoned and demolished by bombing from an American B-1 bomber. Hollywood later made a film, *The Outpost* (2020), based on the incident.

OPPOSITE:
FIREFIGHT
US Army soldiers relax and take a smoke following a firefight with Taliban insurgents on 28 October 2008. The Korengal Valley in eastern Afghanistan was the site of some of the heaviest fighting during the war.

Unmanned aerial vehicles ('drones') offered one possible solution. They were piloted remotely from bases as far away as Saudi Arabia – even the United States itself. The Americans had been using them in Afghanistan from early on, at first chiefly for surveillance. However, over the years of the Bush administration, the number of missile strikes launched from drones had gradually increased. These were targeted at suspected insurgent positions in the remotest and most mountainous eastern regions of Afghanistan – and across the border in Pakistan.

By 2007, however, drone attacks on Pakistan were still in single figures, even if the number rose to 36 in Bush's final year. Again, then, Obama was doubling down on an already established strategy when he authorized 54 strikes in his first year. That August, Baitullah Mehsud, a founder of the Pakistani Taliban, was killed in one such strike, causing a major blow to the insurgents and their cause. In 2010 the number of drone attacks shot up again to 122, although after that it fell away again.

COMRADE IN ARMS
A soldier of the Afghan National Army (foreground right) fights alongside 1st Battalion The Rifles (1 Rifles), in Nawa, Helmand province, during Operation Tor Tapus, March 2009. The British riflemen were part of the Operational Mentor Liaison Teams (OMLTs) that worked with Afghan army forces to bring them on.

SUSPECTED IMPROVISED EXPLOSIVE DEVICE
British soldiers of 2nd Battalion The Rifles (2 Rifles) mount a 20-hour operation to clear a safe route to Patrol Base Wishton in Sangin, Afghanistan.

ANOTHER CASUALTY
Comrades carry the coffin of Corporal Jonathan Horne of 2nd Battalion The Rifles at his funeral in Walsall, England. Horne was one of five men killed on a patrol near Sangin, Helmand province, in July 2009. Such losses seemed likely to erode public support for the war in Afghanistan.

The reason wasn't far to find: the precision of the drones, the pinpoint accuracy of their missile strikes was as impressive as had been claimed. However, they still had to be guided by humans – and distance arguably made their pilots emotionally remote. As with the air strikes, civilians ended up being inadvertently slaughtered. 'Only' 16 in Pakistan in 2010 – not so bad, considering the 788 insurgents killed (or so it seemed from thousands of miles away in the United States) – but the figure was up to 62 the following year.

DRONE DILEMMAS

Inevitably, moreover, the US assessment of who was an insurgent and who a civilian would be disputed. Often, it emerged, zones were identified in which every human present was classed as a 'militant' – even if they were innocent wives or children, or simply bystanders. In some cases, neighbours rushing to assist the victims of one attack were then subjected to a second. Even when the Americans weren't lying, it appeared, they weren't telling the truth.

Ethics apart, the strategy could be counterproductive – despite scoring certain undoubted coups. Baitullah Mehsud's deputy

and successor as leader of the Pakistan Taliban, Hakimullah Meshud, was killed in 2013; Akhtar Mansour, the Afghan Taliban leader, would be 'taken out' in 2016.

BRUTAL BLOWBACK

Nonetheless, many young men were prompted to join the insurgents specifically by the grief and anger they experienced after such attacks. The drones were as decisive in stoking as in suppressing the insurrection.

As were such American 'counterterrorism' measures that included the abduction, indefinite detention and (alleged) torture of suspected militants. Atrocities ranged from the mass executions of prisoners to random massacres of civilian communities, with miscellaneous rapes and beatings in between.

Not that the Taliban could claim to occupy the moral high ground. Their entire military methodology relied on the use of terror. 'Collateral' casualties were hardly collateral at all to the IEDs and suicide bombings they employed. These civilian deaths sent a potent message from the Taliban to ordinary Afghans. Torture, beatings and massacres were routine, and according to a UN report in 2009 the insurgents were responsible for most civilian deaths. Nor was the Taliban's piety and puritanism enough to make them shy away from the mass rape of women in territories they took.

SILVER LININGS

There were abuses and atrocities on both sides, but the one great constant was that ordinary Afghan people bore the brunt. They were having a terrible time and would have been unlikely to react warmly to being told

MOUNTAIN PATROL
A French soldier walks away from an Afghan National Army pick-up truck in the spectacular surroundings of Wardak province in July 2009.

that, by certain measures, their lives were objectively getting better. They were, however, and remarkably rapidly. The foreign aid hadn't been entirely wasted: between the effects of infrastructural upgrading and of a partial peace, the economy had in fact been growing more robust.

There had also been sustained investment in education and healthcare; progress had been dramatic in both. In 2001, only a million Afghan children had been enrolled in primary school; by 2010 the figure was approaching 7 million. This was a vast improvement for boys' education, but it was utterly transformative for girls – most of whom had historically received no schooling of any kind. By 2010, 37 per cent did – a dismal rate by the standards of the developed world, but an immeasurably important breakthrough for Afghanistan.

Life expectancy at birth in 2001 had been just under 57. By 2010, that figure had gone up to 66. As ever, the key determinant was infant mortality. This had been heading in the opposite direction, falling from 89.26 deaths per 1000 live births in 2001 to 67.36 in 2010.

OPPOSITE ABOVE:
ANGELA-APPROVED
German Chancellor Angela Merkel lends her influence to Hamid Karzai in the run-up to the Afghan presidential election of 2009.

OPPOSITE BELOW:
INTERNATIONAL STATESMEN
Hamid Karzai enjoys the hospitality of Barack Obama in the White House during a trilateral meeting with Pakistani President Asif Ali Zardari on 6 May 2009.

With daily violence and disruption on the one hand and incremental overall improvement on the other, Afghanistan presented a mixed – and in many ways confusing – picture. As did the presidential poll of 20 August 2009, in which Hamid Karzai had to submit himself to the people for re-election. (He should have done so some months earlier, according to the country's constitution, critics claimed.) Inspiring as it was to see Afghans streaming out to vote once more, the conduct of the election was unusual, to say the least.

ELECTION MISCONDUCT

The run-up was marred by accusations of bullying and bribery by government officials. State TV became an arm of the Karzai campaign and his opponent Abdullah Abdullah could barely get a look in. Local warlords agreed to trade their clients' votes in blocks for ministerial positions. Votes were openly bought and sold and large numbers conjured up from nowhere, in the names of non-existent voters.

When election day came, thousands were prevented from voting by insurgent threats and attacks on polling stations. They hadn't wanted the poll to go ahead. Their intimidation helped Karzai, whose supporters had already sewn up huge quantities of votes, but the militants weren't too worried. If they couldn't stop democracy, they would settle for seeing it discredited, and Afghanistan's continuing status as a 'failed state' underlined.

The violence also prevented international observers from policing what took place. This appears to have included further intimidation and the disappearance of large quantities of ballot papers. Again, this almost certainly assisted the incumbent.

ON THE FIRING RANGE
Female recruits to the Afghan National Police train in the use of the AMD-65 (a Hungarian version of the AK-47) as part of their basic training in 2010. As radical as a decade's changes had been for Afghanistan in general, they'd been truly revolutionary for the country's women.

LEFT:
HEROIN HAUL
A police officer displays seized heroin. Afghanistan is the world's biggest producer of opium, which is refined to make heroin. A symbiotic relationship grew between the illegal drug trade and the Taliban insurgency.

BELOW:
POLICE ACTION
An Afghan police officer watches as 18 tonnes of drugs burn at Lashkar Gah, following successful raids.

OPPOSITE ABOVE:
MARIJUANA FIELD
US soldiers walk through a marijuana field during a patrol in Siah Choy village, Kandahar province, in October 2010.

OPPOSITE BELOW:
ADDICTS
Afghan addicts smoke, freebase and inject heroin in a basement room of the infamous Russian Cultural Center in Kabul.

Hamid Karzai came out on top – 49 per cent to Abdullah's 30. The loser refused to take part in a second-round run-off that the Western powers hoped would retroactively legitimize the whole proceedings, so Karzai was re-elected, triumphant – if somewhat tarnished. His return to the Arg, Afghanistan's presidential palace, underlined the fact that Afghans were back in charge of their own country. At least, it suited both the president and his foreign sponsors for it to be thought so. Karzai wanted to sidestep sneering accusations that he was a puppet of the West; America and its allies the suspicion that the war would never end.

A DECADE ON

Almost a decade had now elapsed since the terrible events of 9/11. The attacks were still, of course, remembered, but they were gradually becoming commemorated in a more ritualistic way. A replacement for the World Trade Center in New York City had been under construction since 2006, although the National September 11 Memorial wasn't to officially open until 11 September 2011. The face of Osama bin Laden had attained iconic status – even if through much of the world it was regarded as an emblem of the utmost evil. US intelligence was leading an international manhunt for the al-Qaeda founder – so far, however, without success.

At a more raw and human level, the memory of the attacks showed signs of fading. Voters in the United States and other Western democracies struggled to understand why their troops were still in Afghanistan. Families wondered why their sons and daughters, serving there, were still having to risk – and

still, too often, lose – their lives. And all for what appeared to be a corrupt and ineffective Afghan state.

The passing years had meanwhile brought new preoccupations and new priorities. To some extent the Afghanistan conflict had been upstaged by the war in Iraq – just as President Obama had feared it would be. If Americans wanted to see blood and horror they could look across their southern border to Mexico, where tens of thousands were dying in a war between the drugs cartels and the authorities there.

PROBLEMS AT HOME

Or they could look closer to home. America had outrages of its own, not least the continuing frequency of its signature spree shootings. In 2007, at Virginia Tech in Blacksburg, undergraduate student Seung-Hui Cho had killed 33 faculty and fellow students, leaving 17 more injured. A quite different kind of destruction had been dealt by the 2008 stock market crash. The prospect of a second 'Great Depression' loomed.

OPPOSITE ABOVE:
POLICING PERFORMANCE
Afghan National policemen carry out a mock arrest of suspects during a capabilities event.

OPPOSITE BELOW:
WORKING FOR YOU
British-trained officers of the Afghan National Police demonstrate a vehicle search. This sort of show, in addition to offering an exciting spectacle, reassured the public that their police force were protecting them.

OVERLEAF:
BOMB SEARCH
Soldiers of the Afghan National Army search a road in Helmand for IEDs. Increasingly, ISAF-trained Afghans were taking over defensive duties.

With such a wide array of anxieties to choose from, America's politicians actually found al-Qaeda – being emblematic of all the United States defined itself against – a convenient focus at election time. Osama bin Laden served a function as the personification of all evil. 'We will kill bin Laden. We will crush bin Laden,' Obama said.

Throughout much of the Muslim world – and to some extent in developing countries more generally – the legacy of 9/11 was complicated in other ways. Vanishingly few may actually have approved of the atrocity, but many felt a sneaking excitement at the blow it had dealt what they considered an overbearing United States.

Pakistan was particularly ambivalent. Officially a US ally, it had joined in the general condemnation of the 9/11 attacks. How could it not have done? However, Islamabad had

DAWN PATROL
Afghan commandos together with US Special Forces await movement at sunset to remote villages along the Afghanistan and Pakistan border in the Dand Patan district of Paktia province in November 2010.

naturally been uncomfortable with subsequent US-backed ground operations and drone attacks on its territory. Especially when these claimed civilian casualties.

Meanwhile, Pakistani intelligence had its own priorities. Wary as it was of al-Qaeda's ability to stir up radical unrest, especially in its own wild north-west, it couldn't help feeling intrigued by the possibilities it saw for using the group to advance its own agenda in Afghanistan.

OSAMA UPDATE
President Obama and Vice President Joe Biden – along with members of the National Security team, including Hillary Clinton – receive an update on the hunt for Osama bin Laden on 1 May. A classified document in this picture has been obscured, so sensitive does this subject still remain.

As for Osama bin Laden: he may have been a mass murderer and potentially a political threat to the Pakistan government, but at the same time he would have been a handy card for any player to have up their sleeve in the great geopolitical poker game.

Hence the speculation (indignantly denied) that Islamabad was already aware of bin Laden's whereabouts in May 2011 when the Americans tracked him down. Until then believed to be lying low in the semi-autonomous Federally Administered Tribal Areas, up by the Afghan border, he turned out to be hiding in the town of Abbottabad, well to the east.

Here he was killed in a raid by US Navy SEALs who had been flown in by two Black Hawk helicopters from just over the Afghan border in Jalalabad, having previously travelled from Virginia, via Germany and Bagram Airbase. Led to its location by informants and by evidence received from secret wiretaps, the Americans had been watching the Abbottabad compound in which bin Laden was hiding from surveillance drones.

A missile strike from a drone would have been the obvious way of 'taking out' the terrorist. This option was seriously considered, despite it involving an attack in a nominally friendly country, which would almost inevitably involve civilian casualties.

DEADLY DILEMMAS

The risk of harming bin Laden's staff wasn't going to worry the Obama administration. The killing of their families – innocent women and children – might even be justified, but how many deaths could be defended? What if neighbours unconnected to al-Qaeda were killed or wounded? How would this be explained to Pakistan and the wider Muslim world? The possibility that there might be an armoured bunker beneath the compound meant that a big and powerful warhead would be required. However precisely this was targeted, its blast-circumference was bound to be such as to put a number of neighbouring properties at risk.

Even these considerations might not have been sufficient to dissuade the Americans, bent on vengeance. A less fastidious objection stayed their hand. Should bin Laden be immolated in his hideout, where would be the proof that he had been killed? How was the spectre of his reputation to be put to rest?

Hence, the hands-on human approach. After a series of rehearsals in a carefully built mock-up in Nevada, the SEALs were able to take over the compound in a matter of minutes. Bin Laden and four of his men were killed before the SEALs made their escape and 17 bin Laden supporters were subsequently arrested by the Pakistani authorities.

OPPOSITE ABOVE:
INCOGNITO
Behind the blank walls of this anonymous compound – less than a couple of kilometres from the Pakistan Military Academy – stands the Abbottabad townhouse in which Osama bin Laden spent his final days.

OPPOSITE BELOW:
'BIN LADEN IS THERE'
Jessica Chastain stars as Maya, a fictional CIA analyst, in the action thriller *Zero Dark Thirty* (2012). The film's success confirmed that the hunt for Osama bin Laden had become part of modern mythology.

OVERLEAF:
NOTHING TO SEE HERE
Wary-looking Pakistani policemen stand guard outside the last hideout of Osama bin Laden shortly after his death. Officially, Islamabad had been unaware of his whereabouts in Pakistan; inevitably, however, Western analysts have had their doubts.

ERASING THE RECORD
The Abbottabad house in which Bin Laden died was promptly demolished by the authorities, anxious to erase all signs of his presence there. His body was buried at sea – a slight, but also American claimed, a precaution against his grave becoming an Islamist shrine. Inevitably, there were suspicions of some (unspecified) darker motive.

BLOODY RESURGENCE

The killing of Osama bin Laden was a considerable coup for the Americans, but it didn't bring the closure they had hoped for. Partly, because the circumstances of his death seemed so uncertain – and they themselves were so loath to quell the doubts. The al-Qaeda leader had been shot dead, although he was reportedly unarmed. Then there had been the hugger-mugger haste in which they had disposed of the body. What, some wondered, were the Americans trying to hide?

Tempting as it was to announce the end of an era, the reality was only too clearly otherwise. Just five days later, on 7 May, the Battle of Kandahar began. A grandiose title for an assault by a few hundred insurgents who were beaten back by the southern city's ANA garrison with British help. With eight deaths on the victorious government side and only 25 on the Taliban's, this couldn't be called a historic confrontation. Yet, it was still significant. As we've already seen, 'asymmetric warfare' comes with asymmetric expectations.

OPPOSITE:
CHINOOK PATROL
RAF Chinooks take off from Camp Bastion airfield in Helmand province. Osama bin Laden might be dead, but the insurgency in Afghan was showing no sign of letting up and ISAF (International Security Assistance Force) operations had to continue as before.

ALL PHOTOGRAPHS:
BOOTS ON THE GROUND

The second half of 2011 was a dangerous time for America and its ISAF allies, both militarily and politically. The insurgents had doubled down on their commitment, conscious that the USA had achieved a coup with bin Laden's killing and eager to prove that they had not been weakened by his death.

Meanwhile, the Americans were anxious to show that their 'surge' was gaining traction and that forces were making progress on the ground. Realistically, this meant personnel putting themselves in harm's way in the field of battle. To be genuinely useful, even air strikes had to be planned and coordinated from the ground (left). The basic stuff of soldiering entailed trudging across often difficult terrain (opposite). It was the same for the Afghan National Army with ISAF (below).

BACK TO BASICS
US Marines patrol an open area in Nawa, Helmand province. Difficult conditions on the ground did much to level the battlefield for the insurgents.

MURDER BY MISSILE
The drone-fired missiles that
hit houses in the Pakistani
tribal area of North Waziristan
on 13 October 2011 killed
ten militants, including a
commander of the al-Qaeda-
linked Haqqani group. Yet
Islamist protesters, like these in
Multan, Punjab, pointed to the
civilian casualties such strikes
so often caused. What was this,
they asked, but US terrorism?

Despite an overwhelming superiority in strength, the great power (especially a democratic power, with a free and voluble media) is ill-equipped to tolerate setbacks of any sort.

Kandahar's defenders finally sent the insurgents packing, but it took them two days' of fierce fighting. Regardless of the result, the American public were disconcerted to see the Taliban still in business, still capable of mounting a significant attack.

ASYMMETRIC AIMS

For many Americans, the removal of Osama bin Laden meant that the justification for the war had largely gone. Another important asymmetry, it might be felt. The Western public had been encouraged to see the war as being all about 9/11 and al-Qaeda, but that was a side issue for the insurgents. Bin Laden's death had been no real loss to them. Essentially, the al-Qaeda leader and his staff had been (paying) guests of their government. The Taliban felt a certain hostly loyalty, but had never signed up to their grander plans. Al-Qaeda's aspiration had been to bring the Muslim world together in a single, overarching state or caliphate. Proudly parochial, the

Taliban scorned utopianism of this sort. As for the United States and the West, while despising them for their decadence, and determined not to be seen to buckle to their bullying, they had felt no deeper animus than that.

REVERSING THE SURGE

The killing of Osama bin Laden had been a sideshow for America's government too, in fact. Eighteen months had passed since the start of the 'surge'; by President Obama's optimistic initial timetable, they should largely have achieved their aims and been ready to start returning home.

OPPOSITE & ABOVE:
INFLAMMATORY SITUATION
Raymond Allen Davis (left)is conducted to a court appearance in Lahore on 28 January 2011. A former US soldier and freelance security agent, Davis admitted shooting dead two men, although he insisted he had done so in self-defence. Many Pakistanis weren't persuaded. Protesters outside the courthouse (above) shout slogans and set fire to a mock US flag. Although US pressure at first only stiffened the Pakistani authorities' resolve, they eventually agreed that the charges could be dismissed once compensation had been paid to the two men's families.

DOZER IN ACTION

US combat engineers work through the night demolishing Firebase Saenz, a patrol base in Helmand province – the first of many such installations to be 'demilitarized' in December 2011. The lurid light lends the scene a hellish aspect, but then Afghanistan was as infernal as ever. This may have been a drawdown, but it wasn't peace.

On the ground, however, conditions continued to be trying. Obama had little choice politically that June but to announce a drawdown of 10,000 troops by the end of 2011, and of 23,000 more by mid-2012. His allies announced comparable reductions. In fact, Canada had withdrawn the bulk of its 3000 combat troops by the beginning of July, leaving just a few hundred on training duties with the Afghan National Army (ANA).

The idea of handing over combat duties to the ANA had been an objective of the West for some time – albeit an elusive Holy Grail. Now, polls were revealing a growing war-weariness among their electors, and governments redoubled their efforts to find a way of stepping back.

AN ADVANTAGEOUS SITUATION

Meanwhile, the fighting in the countryside continued, bloody as ever. The Americans still had to take the lead; its ISAF (International Security Assistance Force) allies for the most part were still fighting. Despite the politicians' public optimism, progress remained slow – and by no means always steady – against what

analysts were calling a 'resilient insurgency'. For, if the Taliban couldn't strike a killer blow, they were fully capable of launching small-scale local attacks: more than 20,000 in 2011. Mere irritants, mostly, to the Western forces, though far more than that to Afghan civilians still dying in their thousands at the insurgents' hands each year. Nor, despite what was on the face of it their overwhelming military superiority, were the Americans managing to find a way of winning.

ABOVE:
IN ACTION
Afghan soldiers prepare to board an MI-17 helicopter for air insertion training in southern Kandahar province, March 2012. From this time, the Afghan National Army (ANA) was going to have to lead the fight against the insurgency: this meant undertaking tough and complex operations.

OPPOSITE ABOVE:
RIFLE-READY
A member of the Afghan National Police waits to take apart his assault rifle during weapons training in December 2012. Speed in stripping and cleaning a rifle is an essential skill for the modern soldier.

OPPOSITE BELOW:
AFGHAN ARMY PATROL
ANA soldiers await the order to move out on a clearing operation in Trek Nawa, Helmand province, April 2012.

ON THE EDGE
An armed policeman stands guard at Kabul's police headquarters, following the fatal shooting of a US civilian advisor by a female Afghan officer on 24 December 2012. The incident raised alarming questions as to the loyalty of Afghan security forces at a time when they were being asked to shoulder more of the responsibility for keeping the country safe.

BORDER CROSSING

The insurgents were still taking advantage of the proximity of the Pakistani border. They could go back and forth at will, resting up in camps in the tribal areas – perhaps with the tacit support of Pakistani intelligence. While US drones did score some hits on these insurgent bases, they also caused civilian casualties. The inevitable backlash put political pressure on the Americans to curtail these strikes. Overall, civilian casualties appeared to have peaked, although with 2769 recorded in 2012 the number remained horrifically high. Comparatively few were down to the ISAF – although those that were made international headlines.

And rightly so. They included February's Kapisa air strike in which a NATO attack on a village in that province killed seven children and one 'adult' (an 18-year-old mentally impaired youth), and the so-called 'Kandahar massacre' in March. Here a US Army Staff

ABOVE:
V-22 OSPREY TILTROTOR
Members of II Squadron RAF Regiment and the US Marines board an Osprey aircraft at Camp Bastion during Operation Backfoot, a combined coalition operation to disrupt insurgent activity in Helmand province.

OPPOSITE ABOVE:
BITTER BEREAVEMENT
Family, friends and comrades look on as the coffin of Sergeant Gareth Thursby leaves RAF Brize Norton, England. Every death in war is tragic, but the Yorkshireman's seemed particularly pointless. Sergeant Thursby represented a new kind of casualty for the coalition – killed in a 'green on blue' (or 'insider') attack by an Afghan National Army recruit.

OPPOSITE BELOW:
NEVER FORGOTTEN
At the National Cemetery in Arlington, Virginia, on Memorial Day 2012, Karen Clarkson mourns her son Joel, an Army Ranger killed in action in Afghanistan two years earlier. America, a wealthy superpower, could sustain the war indefinitely, but the human cost was rising by the month.

Sergeant 'went rogue', killing 16 civilians and wounding six others – in 'revenge' for a recent IED attack.

PARTNERS FOR PEACE
NATO Secretary General
Anders Fogh Rasmussen and
Senior Civilian Representative
Simon Gass arrive at Camp
Moorhead, near Kabul, for
talks with Hamid Karzai in
April 2012. All sides agreed to
work for 'an Afghanistan with
Afghans fully in charge of their
own security by the end of 2014'.

IN RESERVE
Maintenance checks are carried out by US soldiers on an M1A1 Abrams tank at Camp Shir Ghazay, Helmand province in April 2013. By this time, combat duties had been handed over to the Afghan National Army, but 100,000 ISAF troops remained in the country with all their kit.

SCRAMBLE!
The 31 Squadron aircrew for a Royal Air Force Tornado GR4 multirole fighter scramble to their aircraft at Kandahar airfield to support troops on the ground in Helmand province. The Afghan National Army may have taken over combat duties on the ground, but it still needed cover from the air.

Several subsequent NATO air strikes claimed civilian casualties as the year went on: three shopkeepers dying in one attack in July and eight women in another in Laghman, eastern Afghanistan, in September.

That the Taliban were killing far more – exacting a daily attrition with their IEDs, suicide attacks and targeted assassinations – did not absolve the West of its responsibility. It did, however, underline the ineffectiveness of an ISAF approach that couldn't seem to do more than contain the insurgency. An insurgency whose 'resilience' only seemed to be deepening, not surprisingly when it was, by now, the main employer in much of the country. A fighter's pay was better than a farmer's.

The remoter regions of Afghanistan were also in semi-anarchy: after fighting, the main economic activity was opium cultivation. Even in nominally Kabul-controlled areas, the government's attempted crackdown had limited success; beyond these the drugs gangs had free rein.

ABOVE:
COVERING FIRE
A British Royal Artillery corporal covers comrades as they advance across open ground in Helmand's Upper Gereshk Valley during Operation Qalb (Heart) in 2012. The operation's aim was to find arms caches and drive away insurgents from the vicinity of Highway 1, Afghanistan's main ring road.

OPPOSITE BOTH PHOTOGRAPHS:
STRIKING AT THE ROOTS
A soldier searches the home of a Taliban leader captured in Khugyani, Nangarhar, in eastern Afghanistan (opposite below). Afghan troops take the lead in the raid (top). The arrest was important as he had played a key role in radicalizing, recruiting and training new fighters and suicide bombers for the insurgent cause. As so often is the case, the grief and anger many young Afghans felt spurred their recruitment. 'Counterterrorism' could be counterproductive, it was clear.

Some observers suggested that the 'resilience' of the uprising might be attributable in part to President Bush's decision to invade Iraq. President Obama had long been of this

ABOVE:
AN UNAVAILING STRUGGLE
An Afghan policeman cuts a quixotic figure as he takes a
stick to a field of poppies in the far north-eastern province
of Badakshan. The trade in opium had come to underpin
the Taliban economy, but official attempts to eradicate it
proved ineffective.

OPPOSITE:
A NATION IN TRAUMA
Nine-year-old Nabila Rehman holds up a picture she has
drawn of the drone strike that killed her grandmother. The
remote-control warfare the drones represented naturally
appealed to the United States because it spared their
soldiers. The campaigners who set up this news conference
in Washington DC on 29 October 2013, wanted to remind
Americans of the human cost.

view. Not just because the second war had
drawn attention and resources away from the
first, but because the regional instability that the
two had collectively created had contributed to
the sort of pan-Islamic radicalism the West was
supposed to have been fighting.

As we have seen, the Taliban had shown
little interest in the idea that their religious

path might have an internationalist dimension.
Nor, not being Arabs, could they get behind
al-Qaeda's ambitions for a caliphate (a state
governed in accordance with Islamic law)
across the Arab world.

Some in Afghanistan could, however, and
they were inspired by those Iraqi radicals who
had from 2014 been fighting the Americans
as 'Islamic State' (IS). (The group had existed
since 1999 but the invasion of Iraq had given it
a new purpose.) In parts of eastern Afghanistan,
IS set itself up in opposition to the Taliban – if
not in government, then in a dominating role.
However, its Taliban enemy's enemy was no
friend to the United States. Even less so after
13 April 2017.

On that day in Nangarhar, eastern
Afghanistan, the Americans dropped their
biggest non-nuclear bomb – the GBU-43/B
Massive Ordnance Air Blast (MOAB) – on an
IS headquarters in a cave complex. The attack
killed 96 militants. Without, however, ending
the insurgency.

ABOVE:
DISPUTED DEMOCRACY
Afghan elections had already gained a reputation for chicanery and violence – and 2014 was no exception. US Secretary of State John Kerry had to mediate between rivals Abdullah Abdullah (left) and Ashraf Ghani (right). They eventually formed a unity government, with Ghani as president and Abdullah as chief executive.

RIGHT:
A CONTROVERSIAL CASE
For reasons that remain unclear, US soldier Beaudry 'Bowe' Bergdahl deserted his post in 2009 and was taken captive by al-Qaeda-aligned Haqqani fighters. He was freed in a prisoner exchange in 2014.

OPPOSITE:
AN END IN SIGHT
President Barack Obama walks into the White House Rose Garden on 27 May 2014 to announce his plan to withdraw all US combat troops from Afghanistan by the end of 2016.

BLESSING
A priest blesses soldiers at Tbilisi's Vaziani base before their departure to join the Resolute Support Mission (RSM) in March 2015. Replacing the International Security Assistance Force (ISAF), the RSM was primarily geared to train Afghan forces rather than to fight. For Georgia, a former-Soviet state, participation was an opportunity to demonstrate its good faith and readiness to assist those it hoped would, before too long, be its NATO partners.

COLLATERAL CARNAGE

A decade and a half after the US air strike that crushed the Kandahar clinic, another destroyed the Médecins Sans Frontières (Doctors Without Borders) hospital in Kunduz, northern Afghanistan. The attack, on 3 October 2015, which killed 22 and injured many more, left a vital medical installation a smoking ruin. There had always been cynics about the US intervention in Afghanistan, but even ardent supporters of Operation Enduring Freedom found scenes like this one – and there were far too many – dispiriting.

MORE TROOPS IN

Since January 2017, the United States had been in the charge of a new president, Donald Trump. His impatience with what previous administrations had regarded as their country's international obligations had been crucial to his electoral success. Despite this, on assuming office he'd immediately sent more US troops to Afghanistan.

Their efforts were directed firmly into the training of Afghan troops to take their place. Again, this was to prove an uphill struggle. Afghan recruits weren't weak or cowardly: understandably, however, their loyalties were conflicted. Their motives were often mixed, their political priorities not necessarily Washington's – or even Kabul's.

Air attacks on the opium crop scored important hits – but only locally. Afghanistan is a big country and the areas under poppy cultivation were vast. The justification for the campaign was that it would blow up the Taliban's finances, but you couldn't really hope to defeat an enemy by bombing fields.

The Taliban could tell that Trump was even more concerned than his predecessors to keep American soldiers safe. In 2018, the insurgents stepped up their campaign of terror. More than 115 people were killed in a wave of attacks in the capital Kabul.

AFGHAN AIR FORCE
An A-29 Super Tucano – a light attack aircraft – on a training mission in April 2016. Efforts from early on to bring Afghan troops into the conflict on the ground had proven to be a struggle, but the building of an air force had been a project for the longer term. Major investment in money, equipment and training, as well as a sustained period of stability, were required. NATO's Train, Advise and Assist Command – Air teams worked with the Afghans to bring this about from 2015.

BEFORE THE BLAST

A prototype GBU-43/B Massive Ordnance Air Blast (MOAB) bomb captured in the moment before its explosive impact in a test on 11 March 2003. The mushroom cloud could be seen from 32km (20mi) away.

FROM CAVES TO CRATERS

An aerial photograph reveals the damage done by the GBU-43/B MOAB dropped on Islamic State's headquarters in a Nangarhar cave complex on 13 April 2017. America's superpower strength had frequently been thwarted in Afghanistan: one of the ironies of 'asymmetric warfare'. On occasion, however, its sheer firepower paid off.

TRUMP SPEAKS

President Donald Trump is interviewed in the Oval Office on 1 May 2017. He would succeed where his predecessors had failed in getting American forces out of Afghanistan, but would do so at untold cost to that country.

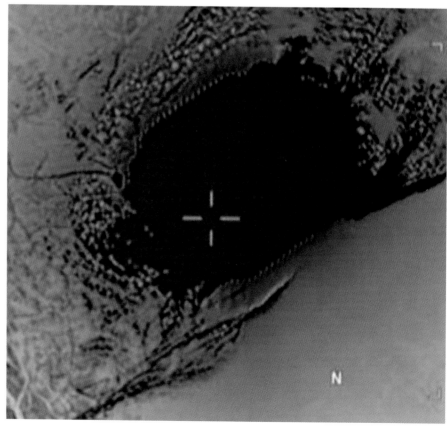

TARGET THE CHILDREN
Afghan officials inspect the damage caused by an Islamic State attack on a compound belonging to the British NGO Save the Children in Jalalabad, Nangarhar, in 2018. Three staff members were killed.

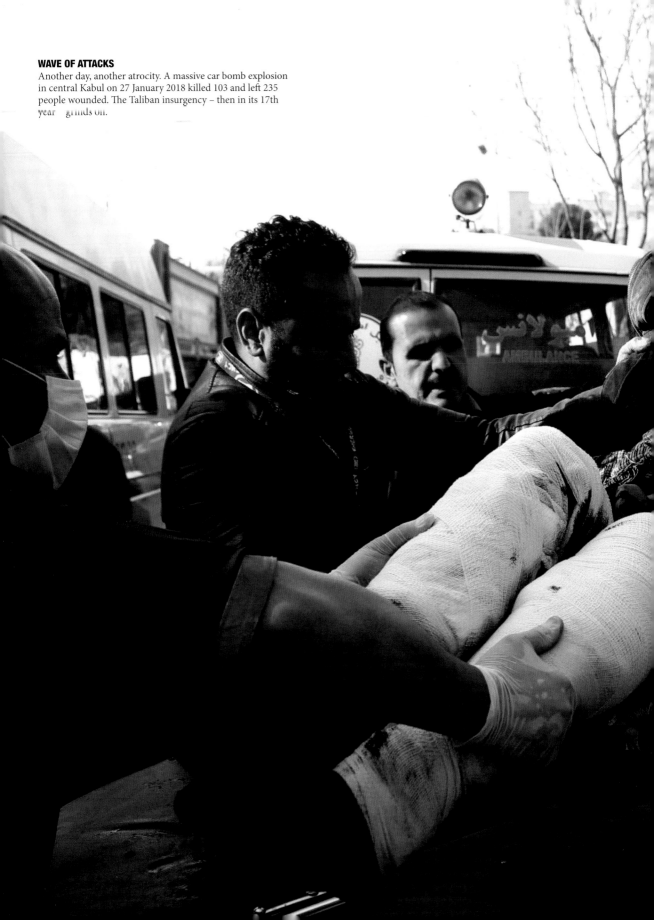

WAVE OF ATTACKS

Another day, another atrocity. A massive car bomb explosion in central Kabul on 27 January 2018 killed 103 and left 235 people wounded. The Taliban insurgency – then in its 17th year – grinds on.

OPPOSITE TOP:
DANISH CONTINGENT
Danish soldiers stand in formation at Camp Viking in Helmand province on 20 May 2014 during the ceremony marking the end of Danish combat operations.

OPPOSITE BOTTOM:
RAF WITHDRAW
Personnel from 904 Expeditionary Air Wing and the Joint Force Support Unit based at Kandahar Airfield board a C17 aircraft bound for the UK.

ABOVE:
CASUALTY EVACUATION
C-130 Hercules engines start up before carrying out another Afghan air force casualty evacuation mission in June 2014.

LEFT:
CAMP BASTION TRANSFER
A piper with 4th Scots is pictured playing the bagpipes following a transfer of authority ceremony between his unit and 5th Rifles at Camp Bastion in May 2014.

WITHDRAWAL

Decenber 2019 marked the 40th anniversary of the Soviet invasion of Afghanistan. Few felt inclined to celebrate it. Certainly not the US media, which back in 1979 had excitedly entertained the hope that this conflict could prove to be 'Russia's Vietnam'.

The US war in Vietnam (1955–73) became the kind of 'quagmire' that Defense Secretary Donald Rumsfeld 'didn't do' (he was to ban Pentagon staff from using the word during the Iraq war). Almost certainly the specific quagmire the Defense

Secretary had in mind, Vietnam had turned out to be totally traumatic for America.

Critics have queued up to deride the claim that Vietnam had been an 'American tragedy', pointing out that US losses (over 58,000) had been only around a fifth those of its South Vietnamese allies. The Communist Vietnamese (North Vietnamese Army and South Vietnamese Viet Cong guerrillas) had lost well over a million combatants, while anything up to 2 million civilians had been killed.

OPPOSITE:
HEADING HOME
President Donald Trump changes planes at Ramstein US Airbase in Germany after a surprise Thanksgiving visit to troops in Afghanistan in November 2019. Soon, he said, they'd be coming home themselves.

LEFT:
ABDUL GHANI BARADAR
A childhood friend of Taliban founder Mullah Omar and a veteran of the war against the Soviets, Abdul Ghani Baradar had been high up in the Taliban hierarchy from the start. After eight years in prison in Pakistan, he returned to the fray in 2019 as, effectively, the movement's leader.

BELOW:
RESOLUTE SUPPORT
From 2015, the NATO-led Operation Resolute Support had set out to train, advise and assist the Afghan National Army and wider security forces in the country. 'Assistance' was broadly defined to include the combat support that US special forces could provide. It also included help with policing, such as this raid in Farah province, south-western Afghanistan, in which a large quantity of drugs and drug-making equipment was seized and destroyed.

ABOVE:

COLLATERAL DAMAGE?

A beggar who lost his leg from a mine injury is seen in Kabul traffic hoping to receive some charity from people driving by. According to the United Nations Assistance Mission in Afghanistan (UNAMA), civilian casualties in 2021 reached record levels, including a particularly sharp increase in killings and injuries since May, when international military forces began their withdrawal and the fighting intensified following the Taliban's offensive. There were 2,392 in total (783 killed and 1,609 injured) for the first six months of the year, the highest since records began in 2009.

Once again, however, the asymmetry was all. Double standards or not, it was how Americans had felt. The Vietnamese on either side had really had no alternative but to be stoical. The US public mourned those they'd lost in a war their governments had chosen to fight – then hadn't won.

They also mourned the wider effects of a conflict that had cost their country dearly – in terms of its reputation abroad and morale at home. America's self-image as a defender of democracy, an upholder of humanity, had been badly dented by reports of atrocities committed by its own forces.

EXIT ISSUES

Ironically, it had only been in so far as the United States had truly been a democracy, however flawed, that these damaging reports had made it home. In the absence of a free press, citizens of the Soviet Union had been left largely in ignorance of their forces' excesses in Afghanistan. Even so, the Soviets' Afghan adventure had been a bruising experience – perhaps even, ultimately, a fateful one – for the Communist superpower.

The lessons of Vietnam, compounded by what had been seen of the Soviet Union's torrid time in Afghanistan, had also been thrown into relief by the Battle of Mogadishu in 1993. The misery that followed America's ill-fated intervention to try to shore up a collapsing Somali state had introduced a new phrase to popular parlance: 'exit strategy'.

America's absolute losses in Somalia had been small – 18 killed and 73 wounded. Again, however, they loomed large for the media and an apparently disaffected US public.

The call for an exit strategy had recurred in discussions about Afghanistan before America's intervention. And while successive administrations had arguably decided to disregard it, they'd invariably been at pains publicly to stress that their commitments to the conflict had been strictly limited in both extent and time.

FIXING A LIMIT

True, in the days of shock that had immediately followed 9/11, George W. Bush had made the open-ended-sounding promise: 'We will not tire'. More measured counsels had quickly prevailed, however. Rumsfeld, we've seen, had been taking steps to dampen expectations since early in 2002; Barack Obama had hedged around his pledge to boost American strength in Afghanistan with assurances that this would be a strategy only for the short term.

The months had turned to years, however, and the sobering reality was that, by the start of 2019, US combat troops had been in Afghanistan for almost two decades. This was twice as long as US forces had been actively engaged in the war in Vietnam (1965–73), and as long as US involvement there had lasted overall (1955–73).

DENIABLE ASSISTANCE
An Afghan soldier cradles
a child in the aftermath of a
suicide bombing in September
2019. Behind him, his face
partly obscured, a US medic
gives help to another soldier.
By this time, American service
personnel had been providing
support in Afghanistan for
almost two decades, but their
government was beginning to
become more cagy.

MODERN MARTYR
A mural commemorates TV presenter turned PR man Yama Siawash who was assassinated in November 2020. To the Taliban-linked Haqqani group he represented the vision of a new, democratic and Western-orientated Afghanistan whose emergence they were committed to suppressing.

OPPOSITE:
MORE OF THE SAME
A shipment of US armoured trucks is unloaded on 13 July 2020. For all Donald Trump's avowals, America's responsibilities in Afghanistan showed no signs of coming to an end.

While the figures for serving Americans lost (in the low thousands) were dwarfed by those from the former conflict, a once-bitten public was twice shy.

From 1969, President Richard Nixon had attempted a policy of 'Vietnamization' – the gradual disengagement of US forces from the fight with the Communists while conduct of the war was handed over to the South Vietnamese.

It had proven neither straightforward nor (ultimately) successful.

As we've seen, the ISAF countries had been trying to achieve something similar in Afghanistan from as early as 2003, if not before. Yet the coalition forces were still there, and still involved.

They had to be. Paradoxically, in fact, their withdrawal would have to be covered by a beefed-up presence in the short term: it didn't look as though the Afghan National Army could keep control. The Western powers were caught in a cleft stick: the tactical case for a continued presence as compelling as the political one for pulling out. So compelling that even the notoriously wayward and wilful Donald Trump was to acknowledge it. On the campaign trail, he had been scathing about the entire US enterprise in Afghanistan. 'No more wasted lives,' he'd said in 2013; 'Rebuild the US first.' American servicemen and women should be immediately withdrawn.

MEDIA TARGET
The blazing car of local journalist Nisar Ahmad Ahmadi after
the explosion of an IED embedded to his vehicle in Lashkar Gah,
Helmand on 12 March 2019. Fortunately, he survived the attack.
In their efforts to forestall the emergence of a free and democratic
Afghanistan, the Taliban and their allies made the press a target.

Even so, once elected president, Trump had faced different realities and felt obliged to raise US troop levels in the country. And by a considerable number: from 8500 when he took office in January 2017 to 14,000 by the beginning of the following year; an increase not far short of 65 per cent. Once again, a leader of the world's outstanding superpower found himself compromised over Afghanistan, torn between existing commitments and his desire to see them end. Brazen insouciance saw President Trump through what might have been a major humiliation, but how long he would be able to shake off the criticism wasn't clear.

Afghan President Ashraf Ghani had for some time seen the writing on the wall. With Western allies looking more unreliable by the month, he had reconciled himself to the idea of making peace with the Taliban, first inviting them to talks at the beginning of 2017. A war-wearied Afghan people appeared willing for him to make whatever compromises might be necessary to bring the decades of bitter conflict to an end. He was imposing no prior conditions on the talks, he promised the Taliban, and offered to release several hundred prisoners to demonstrate goodwill.

RUNNING DOWN THE CLOCK

His enemy saw no compelling reason to meet him halfway, however. Time, the Taliban could see, was on their side. They didn't have to 'win' outright, to bring down Ghani's government – just keep up the heat on Kabul and therefore, indirectly, on Donald Trump. Accordingly, while Ghani strove to reinforce democracy in Afghanistan, the Taliban continued their war of attrition against the country's institutions, killing and intimidating judges, journalists, civil servants and political activists on a daily basis.

PROGRESS PREVENTED

Steps were still being taken by Ghani's government to build the infrastructure that would give Afghanistan at least a chance of making its way in the world as a modern nation. The state signed up together with some of its neighbours to assist with the TAPI (the Turkmenistan–Afghanistan–Pakistan–India) natural gas pipeline and CASA–1000 (the Central Asia–South Asia hydroelectric project). An iron smelter was also built in Kabul, in the hope that one day Afghanistan could be an exporter of steel. A railway line was opened across the border to Turkmenistan, with the prospect in the future of onward connections to the Caucasus and Black Sea.

OPPOSITE ABOVE:
PEACE WITH HONOUR?
US Defense Secretary Mark Esper stands with Afghan President Ashraf Ghani to announce the US–Afghanistan Joint Declaration at the Dilkusha Mansion Garden in Kabul on 29 February 2020. Essentially Trump's deal with the Taliban, it left Ghani isolated and his government in an untenable position for the longer term.

OPPOSITE BELOW:
EMPTY PROMISES
US Special Representative for Afghanistan Reconciliation Zalmay Khalilzad (left) and Taliban leader Abdul Ghani Baradar (right) sign a peace agreement after talks in Dohar, Qatar, on 29 February 2020. The USA pledged to remove its troops from Afghanistan within 14 months; the Taliban promised to cut its links with jihadist terror groups. Since these didn't apparently include the supporters of their own insurgency, this effectively meant Afghanistan's abandonment by the United States and NATO.

LEFT & OPPOSITE:
DRAWDOWN
Aircrew (left) carry their kit
aboard a C-17 Globemaster III
at the Al Udeid Airbase in Qatar,
April 2021, ready to assist in
the safe and orderly evacuation
of US forces from Afghanistan.
Staff stand by (opposite) as a
CH-47 Chinook helicopter is
made secure aboard a C-17
ready for transportation out of
Afghanistan in June 2021.

BELOW:
AIRLIFT
Dazed-looking Afghan soldiers,
two of them wounded, are
whisked away in a UH-60 Black
Hawk helicopter, picked up
from the Shah Wali Kot outpost,
north of Kandahar on 6 May
2021. While Western forces were
still present in Afghanistan, they
were by now few in number and
had one foot out the door – a
door on which the Taliban and
their allies were hammering.
America had been generous in
leaving the Afghan armed forces
planes and helicopters – just as
well, given that the insurgents
now controlled the country's
roads.

AWAITING RESCUE
US Marines oversee the evacuation of designated personnel from Kabul's Hamid Karzai International Airport in the final days before the Taliban fighters take over in August 2021.

However, the insurgents did their best to thwart all these plans. And while the state had set out to cement the rights of women under the Afghan constitution (requiring, for example, that their details be included on their children's identity cards), the opposition kept up a campaign of low-level harassment and bullied them into staying in their homes.

PEACE AT ANY PRICE

If President Ashraf Ghani persisted in his quest for peace, it was with the growing appreciation – on his part and internationally – that any meaningful process would from now on mainly be a matter of managing defeat. With the rug effectively pulled from under him, Ghani had little choice but to go along with the peace deal reached in Doha, Qatar, on 29 February 2020, by the US negotiator Zalmay Khalilzad and the Taliban's Abdul Ghani Baradar.

Under its terms, the United States was going to close five bases and reduce its presence in Afghanistan from 13,000 to 8600 over the next four months. Assuming that the Taliban kept their commitment to cut their links with (vaguely categorized) terrorist organizations, it would withdraw completely by April 2021. NATO pledged to scale down its presence on a similar timetable.

Although the Afghan government had not been involved in the talks, the agreement nevertheless committed it to the release of 5000 Taliban prisoners. An indignant Ghani dragged his feet, but was only delaying the inevitable.

The 'peace' agreement was promptly followed by a dramatic upturn in insurgent activity. The Americans and NATO kept their word. An honourable course? Perhaps, although for Vietnam nostalgists the episode recalled the period after the Paris Peace Accords of 1973. These too had nominally committed both the United States and its enemies to stop fighting, but had been 'honoured' only by an America all too obviously eager to effect an exit. In the months that followed, its Communist enemies had pressed their advantage and ultimately pushed on to win the war.

In Afghanistan too, the enemy fought on as though nothing had changed while America and its NATO allies carried on preparing to withdraw. They did slow down or stall to some extent in reaction to the non-response they saw from the other side. By April 2021, when Western forces should have been gone completely, the Americans still had 2500 service personnel in the country; other NATO members had almost 7000.

But withdrawal had acquired unstoppable momentum. Despite the continuation of hostile action by the Taliban, Trump's successor Joe Biden promised that US withdrawal would be concluded by 31 August.

OPPOSITE TOP:
THE LAST SOLDIER
Major General Chris Donahue, commander of the US Army 82nd Airborne Division, approaches a transport plane about to leave Kabul. He was the final US soldier to leave Afghan soil after completing the emergency evacuation of US citizens and selected Afghan friends, thus winding up two decades of American involvement in Afghanistan.

OPPOSITE BELOW:
INTERRUPTED OBSEQUIES
Mourners look up in anguished alarm as jet fighters circle the hilltop cemetery where they have gathered to bury 10 people (seven of them children) killed by a US drone strike in August 2021.

FLIGHT FROM FEAR
US civilians and Afghan staff sit crammed together on one of the last US flights out of Kabul in August 2021. Many local civilians who had worked for the Americans and other NATO members would be left behind, at the mercy of the Taliban.

'WHATEVER IT TAKES...'
President Joe Biden announces the final withdrawal of US troops from Afghanistan. Biden had been a staunch supporter of the war in Afghanistan to begin with, but became increasingly sceptical as time went on. As president, he delayed the final withdrawal of US troops but had completed it by the end of August 2021.

STUDENTS STILL
Afghan schoolgirls study hard in Herat on 17 August 2021, only days after the Taliban's lightning-speed reconquest of the country.

OPPOSITE:
LAST STAND
Anti-Taliban Afghan fighters stand guard at an outpost in Kotal-e Anjuman in Paryan, Panjshir province in August 2021. Despite their air of defiance, the Afghan resistance had no real alternative but to make the best accommodation they could with the victorious Taliban.

LEFT:
OSAMA'S HEIR
History repeated itself when Osama bin Laden's successor as al-Qaeda leader, Ayman al-Zawahiri found refuge with the Taliban. It did so again when he was killed in a US drone strike on Kabul in July 2022.

As the weeks went by and the end of August approached, the situation seemed to unravel with increasing speed. A bomb outside a Kabul school on 8 May killed over 80 – mostly schoolgirls, but within a fortnight the Americans had left their base in Kandahar. By the beginning of July they were leaving Bagram; meanwhile the Taliban had occupied large areas of land, including key crossings of the country's borders with Tajikistan, Iran and Pakistan.

On 6 August they took Zamraj, capital of the south-western province of Nimroz; three days later they captured Kunduz, in the north. Joe Biden was undeterred. Whether his actions are regarded as weak or resolute, he made it clear that he was sticking to his schedule.

Panic ensued as the cities of Ghazni, Herat, Kandahar, Lashnar Gah and Jalalabad fell in the days that followed. On 15 August, the Taliban took Kabul, and PresidentAshraf Ghani fled. Thousands of others would not have that option. At Kabul Airport, chaos reigned and those who feared for their safety under the Taliban tried desperately to get places on the last flights out.

The war in Afghanistan had started with the bang to end all bangs – 9/11. Now, however, it was ending in a whimper. Worse than that, perhaps, given the recriminations now flying back and forth at the way the West was arguably abandoning a people it had promised to protect.

LEFT IN THE LURCH

Among those left behind by those final flights were Afghan interpreters, office staff and others who had worked with the Americans and their NATO allies. The whole country itself had been left in the lurch, it seemed. Girls and women had seen their lives transformed – now they were abruptly facing a change back, to being closed up in their homes and shut out of school. Unthinkable only a generation before, the new Afghanistan had female judges: now they were in hiding, frightened for their lives.

Yet, within days of the Taliban takeover, Afghanistan's girls and women were marching in protest at the injustices they faced. Despite dire threats, they refused to be intimidated, an example to their country and an inspiration to the whole world.

SUFFER THE CHILDREN
A woman weeps as she cradles a malnourished child at a Kabul hospital in August 2022. Between the sanctions imposed by the Western powers and the Taliban's own efforts to crash the economy, Afghanistan was once more in a desperate state.

EVERYDAY HEROINES

Afghan women protest at the establishment of an all-male and ethnically restricted government in September 2021. Armed resistance might have been crushed, but Afghan civilians, especially women, showed awe-inspiring courage in the face of Taliban tyranny.

Picture Credits